WHAT ARE THEY SAYING ABOUT PAUL?

What Are They Saying About Paul?

Joseph Plevnik, S.J.

PAULIST PRESS
New York/Mahwah

Library of Congress
Catalog Card Number: 85-62964

ISBN: 0-8091-2776-8

Published by Paulist Press
997 Macarthur Boulevard
Mahwah, N.J. 07430

Printed and bound in the
United States of America

Contents

Preface

Of the thirteen letters in the New Testament which begin with "Paul the apostle . . ." or "Paul, Silvanus, Timothy . . ." and the like, modern biblical scholars agree that at least Romans, 1 Corinthians, 2 Corinthians, Galatians, Philippians, 1 Thessalonians and Philemon were written or dictated by Paul himself. The question concerning 2 Thessalonians and Colossians is still unsettled. Many exegetes continue to regard them as genuine Pauline letters, although there is a growing consensus that they are of a later origin and reflect a more developed situation in the Church and a shift in theology. Ephesians is now regarded by most exegetes as belonging to a later date, and there is almost a consensus that the pastorals, that is, 1 Timothy, 2 Timothy and Titus, belong to the Pauline school rather than to the apostle himself.

We do not intend to review here the arguments for and against including the disputed letters among those of Paul. The reader can consult on this point introductions to the New Testament: A. Robert, E. Feuillet, *Introduction to the New Testament* (New York-Rome-Paris-Tournai: Desclée, 1965); W. Kummel, *Introduction to the New Testament* (Nashville-New York: Abingdon, 1975); B. Rigaux, *Letters of Paul Modern Studies* (Chicago: Franciscan Herald, 1968). However, what we have to say concerning the apostle will be based on those letters which have been commonly recognized as his. This is not to say that Pauline

1

thought is not present in other letters as well, whether or not they be genuinely Pauline. We will have to refer also to the Acts of the Apostles, now commonly ascribed to Luke the evangelist. Acts 9 and 13–28 deal with Paul and are clearly of great historical value to us. However, more weight will be given to what the apostle himself says than what Luke reports about him, even though some sections in Acts may be based on Luke's personal reminiscences. Scholars have pointed out that Luke presents Paul's activity from his own theological perspective, which may not always agree with that of the apostle. There is, however, a rough correspondence between Paul's own accounts and those in Acts, although with many discrepancies in detail.

The genuine Pauline letters, as most scholars agree today, were written between the years 50–58 A.D. This is a relatively short period of time, and would hardly allow for any serious development of and major shifts in Paul's theology. If we date the Damascus event around 33–35, it means that these developments must have taken place in the first fifteen years after that date, which, according to Luke, included some missionary activity.

There is a freshness in these letters. The apostle does not, as the gospel writers do, hand down traditional sayings ascribed to Jesus, although there is evidence that he knew some of them and that he incorporated fragments of Church traditions into his letters. For the most part he formulates creatively. His thought is nurtured by his profound understanding of the mystery of Christ and flows from a heart deeply in love with Christ. Some have called Paul a mystic. This may be a misnomer, but it does express his union with the risen Lord, his Master. At the same time it must be stated that he was keenly aware of the problems in his communities. It is these concrete occasions and needs that gave the impetus to his theological reflection.

In these letters we find a theology in the making. The original impulses of Paul's thought had not yet reached a comprehensive synthesis. Though the apostle at times repeats his statements, and on occasion reminds the faithful of what he had already handed down to them, his formulation is almost always fresh and made to fit the new situation.

The themes chosen in this book neither represent the whole of the Pauline theology nor are they presented in an exhaustive fashion. They should, however, give the reader some information about Paul's thought and its echoes in modern scholarship.

We chose the Damascus experience because of its foundational significance. Not that it is the only source of the apostle's theology or his only transcendent experience of Christ. It did not take Paul out of the common experience of faith in the Church nor does it preclude his later theological maturing. It did, however, give him a profound understanding of the mystery of Christ and of the purpose of God's plan in Christ in the light of which he integrated all his subsequent experiences and influences. It is the only explanation of his unique emphasis, in his theology, on the death, resurrection and lordship of Christ and of his position with respect to the law.

The resurrection of Christ and of the faithful had been in focus in the 60's and the 70's. For Paul and for us it is of fundamental importance for faith and an essential part of the gospel. Here we have tried to give what we consider the apostle's thought in its context and some interpretation of it in modern scholarship.

The theme of justification by faith has always been the center of attention in Protestant scholarship and has even recently been the subject of ecumenical discussions. Since the 1960's some important developments have taken place which may be of interest to the reader and which give us hope for eventual agreement across confessional lines.

The reflections on the cross are another central aspect of Paul's gospel. They contain the apostle's profound understanding of this mystery as it affects the situation of the world, the messenger, and the hearer of the word. They disclose his struggle in the service of the gospel and remain a challenge to human ways of thinking and to human values.

Finally, the hope which permeates all these letters is a comprehensive summary of Paul's understanding of the Christ event. It gives the context to everything else. Here we try to bring out the basis, the goal and the subject of hope.

These themes should give some idea of the riches of the apostle's thought. We hope to present them here to the reader in the spirit of Paul, who labored incessantly to extend the knowledge and the love of Christ throughout the world.

1
Paul's Damascus Experience

Paul's life as a Christian and his apostolic ministry began, according to him, and as recounted in Acts, at his encounter with Jesus at Damascus. Since the apostle also refers to this event as the origin of his gospel, scholars have tried to determine its influence on Paul's theology. It seems therefore appropriate that our account of what they say about Paul should begin with this event which loomed so large in his thought and in his entire life.

The Starting Point

There is a variety of opinions in scholarly literature as to what really happened at Damascus. B. Rigaux mentioned and critically assesses such explanations as a psychological crisis, a vision, a mystical experience, a trance, a revelation, a conversion, a call, etc.[1] Lest we become entangled in conflicting terminology at the very outset of our inquiry we shall begin by referring to this happening in Paul's life as the "Damascus experience." This designation is neutral and can be made more precise in the course of our investigation.

The basic texts are Galatians 1, 1 Corinthians 9 and 15, as well as the three accounts of the Damascus episode in Acts 9, 22 and 26.

5

How important is this event for our understanding of the apostle and of his message? What is the extent and nature of its influence on Paul's thought and life? How does it relate to his former life in Tarsus and to his Jewish background? Not all scholars agree that Damascus played a dominating role in his future. Some claim that he had been determined in his thinking and language by his Hellenistic background, others stress his Jewish-Pharisaical upbringing, still others single out the transforming influence of the Damascus experience.

Indeed, there can be little doubt that all these backgrounds left some imprint on the apostle, but the question is: How much? and What kind? Which of them is the key to the Paul we know from his writings?

To start with, we ask: How dominant was the influence of the Hellenistic background on the apostle? J. Jeremias[2] gave a masterful appraisal of the above opinions. According to him, neither Paul's Hellenistic background nor his Jewish upbringing provides the key to his thought and life.

Paul was indeed born in Tarsus in Cilicia, probably in the first years of the Christian era. He no doubt came to know various cults in that Hellenistic city and cultural center, was familiar with emperor worship and probably came in contact with certain philosophical schools there, especially with the Stoics. We can find influences of this background in the apostle's writings.

However, Jeremias maintains, this is offset by two factors. First, Acts 22:3 offers us a reliable tradition, as W.C. van Unnik has established, that Paul lived and received his schooling in Jerusalem. Second, as M. Pohlenz has shown, the apostle betrays at best a superficial acquaintance with the Stoic philosophy. In the words of Jeremias, "Neither the mystery religions nor the emperor cult nor Stoic philosophy nor lastly an alleged pre-Christian Gnosticism constitutes the native soil of the Apostle."[3]

We may add that Paul came from a strict Jewish family living in the diaspora. Tarsus would have had a sizable Jewish colony centered around the synagogue in which Greek was the tongue of worship. The Jewish community would be aware of its unique traditions and would maintain its own way of life in the Gentile surroundings.[4]

According to Jeremias, Judaism was the native soil of the apostle, who recalls in Philippians 3:5 that he is a Hebrew born of Hebrews and that he had been a Pharisee and a zealous follower and proponent of the law (see 2 Cor 11:22; Rom 11:1). Jeremias holds that Paul probably spoke Aramaic and received a rabbinical training under Gamaliel (Acts 22:3). As Galatians 3–4 and Romans 4 indicate, he was familiar with the rabbinical argumentation from the Scriptures and could use it effectively. Above all, the apostle shared in the depth of his being the faith and the piety of his people. It is clear that Jewish scriptures and apocalypticism left deep marks on his thought. "Paul's religious life and his theology are deeply rooted in Jewish piety and in Jewish theology and cannot be understood without taking this root into consideration."[5]

G. Bornkamm discounts Luke's report in Acts 22:3 that Paul was raised in Jerusalem. To him, this is part of Luke's tendency to make the apostle an out-and-out Jew.[6] Perhaps; but agreement with this tendency of Luke does not by itself make Acts 22:3 unhistorical.

Yet, Jeremias maintains, for all this, that the key to Pauline thought is not Judaism but rather the Damascus experience. "Paul is one of those men who have experienced a sharp break with their past. His theology is a theology rooted in a sudden conversion."[7]

To show this, Jeremias offers an extensive list of aspects of Pauline theology which are somehow rooted in the encounter at Damascus. We shall take them up later. We can agree here with the main features of his solution, although Hellenistic influence is probably more extensive than he allows it to be. The apostle is at home not only in rabbinic argumentation but also in Hellenistic rhetoric. As Bornkamm has brought out, the diatribe form, i.e., a lively conversational style in short sentences with direct address taking up the imaginary objections of the opponents, is present in many sections of Pauline writings.[8] There is also evidence of Paul's drawing from Hellenistic thought, but the same writings also clearly reveal that the content of the apostle's message is based on his faith in the God of his fathers and on the Christ event. It was the Damascus episode that shed light on the latter and also brought Paul a new understanding of God and of his plan of salvation.

According to Jeremias, the encounter at Damascus was a conversion experience. This is true, but it is only one aspect of the event and must be related to the apostle's call and to the revelation. Although it left a deep imprint on Paul's writings, it is not the main issue in his theology. It is not what he proclaimed.

Some scholars take exception to the word "conversion" on the grounds that Paul's faith in the God of Israel did not change on that occasion. This is true only up to a point. In that encounter, Paul, who until then did not believe in Jesus as the Christ and in fact persecuted those who did believe, came to know and accept him as the Christ, God's Son and God's agent of salvation. This was a turning point for him and, within these limits, can be regarded as a conversion. He turned to Christ, who became his Lord and Master and the desire of his undying love. By the same token his knowledge and love of God made, in the light of this revelation, a quantum leap from which would emerge his later theological reflection and his gospel.

To discover more about what happened at Damascus, we must now turn to the texts. As we have indicated, we find the information about this in the apostle's own references to it and in Luke's descriptions of it in Acts. All of them have been subjected to critical scrutiny. Scholars give priority of witnessing to Paul's personal recollections; the accounts in Acts are regarded as a secondary source of information. In the wake of form and redaction criticisms, i.e., methodologies which investigate respectively the shape of a tradition in its prior, oral stage of transmission and the writer's own literary and theological contribution, they largely discount the historical reliability of Lukan descriptions. However, the apostle's own references have also been questioned for their historical accuracy. We shall here first take up the Lukan descriptions in Acts.

Luke's Descriptions

Luke gives us three complementary descriptions of the Damascus event in Acts 9:1–19, 22:3–16 and 26:9–17. The first one is a "neutral" report by the evangelist himself, the other two are placed on the lips of Paul. In Acts 22 the apostle defends himself before a hostile Jewish crowd at the temple in Jerusalem, while in Acts 26 he presents his message before the Roman governor Festus and the royal couple Agrippa and Bernice.

The account in Acts 9 has two parts, the appearance of Jesus to Paul and the subsequent appearance of Jesus to the disciple Ananias. In the first section, we hear that Paul, on the way to Damascus to rout out the Christians in that city, has a sudden encounter with Jesus. "A light from heaven flashed about him and he fell to the ground and heard a voice saying to him, 'Saul, Saul, why do you persecute me?' And he said, 'Who are you, Lord?' And he said, 'I am Jesus, whom you are persecuting; but rise and enter the city, and you will be told what you are to do.' " In the second section, the Lord appears to Ananias and tells him to go to Paul, lay his hands on him, heal him and impart to him the Holy Spirit. In the encounter the Lord discloses to Ananias his plans to make Paul his witness before the world.

In Acts 22 we find the same twofold scenario. The dialogue is virtually retained. Here, however, Ananias informs Paul of the Lord's commission. In vv. 17–21 the apostle recounts another experience: While he was praying in the temple, he fell into a trance in which the Lord told him to leave Jerusalem and disclosed to him that he would be sent away to the Gentiles. In Acts 26 the Ananias scene is omitted and the commission becomes part of the dialogue. Accordingly, Paul was told by the Lord himself to witness to this appearance as well as to others he would still receive, and that he would be sent to the Gentiles. We note that Luke's accounts differ from those in Paul in many ways. They are told in a story form that has parallels elsewhere, describe the circumstances, record the dialogue and mention the commission. Each description is made to fit into its appropriate place in Acts.

Most exegetes today agree that Luke had a special interest in giving us the three accounts and in depicting the event as he did. He changed whatever information and tradition he had at his disposal to suit his theological purpose in writing Acts. This brings up the following questions: How much in his accounts comes from Luke himself? How much did he receive from tradition? Does this tradition go back to Paul? Does it agree with the presentation in Paul? How do the three accounts relate to one another?

Some scholars regard all three accounts as Luke's own composition,[9] others hold that Luke drew on three separate traditions.[10] Still others credit certain fragments, especially the dialogue sections, to tradition. G. Lohfink has brought out that these accounts draw heavily on the Old Testament depictions of prophetic vocations,[11] others find parallels in the form in certain Jewish writings (2 Maccabees; Joseph and Asseneth).

We cannot pursue these questions here. Our present concern is to find out to what extent these accounts, whether they be credited mostly to Luke or to a pre-Lukan tradition, agree with those in Paul. J. Munck has brought out the following points of agreement: (a) Paul was totally unprepared for this experience of (b) a direct and sudden intervention of the risen Jesus through which (c) the former persecutor turned to Christ and (d) received his apostolic call and commission.[12]

Some scholars would disagree concerning the last two points. On the basis of Luke's presentation they would allow for a gradual development in Paul the persecutor which led to his conversion. They point out that Acts 22 seems to locate the call at a later time. We shall take up the last point again and comment here only on the conversion of Paul at Damascus.

At this point, it may be useful for the sake of clarity, to distinguish between three levels of explanation: stage I, the historical event itself; stage II, the early oral tradition prior to the composition of Acts; stage III, the accounts in Acts. We are focusing here only on stage III. On this level there can be no doubt that Luke presents the Damascus event as the conversion of Paul. The contexts of the three accounts make this abundantly clear. The persecutor of Christians turned to Christ, joined the faithful and began to preach Christ.

Luke depicts the Damascus experience as a real event in the life of Paul with a profound and lasting effect on the apostle and on the development of the Church. He clearly roots the apostle's proclamation in this encounter. Paul is to witness to all concerning what he heard and saw (Acts 22:15). But the evangelist also integrates Paul into the gradual turning of the Church to the Gentiles. What Peter initiated with Cornelius at Joppa, the apostle of the Gentiles was to take up after Damascus and carry to the ends of the earth. From chapter 13 on, Acts deals almost exclusively with this mission to the Gentiles.

Paul's Accounts

The accounts in Paul provide, from the historian's point of view, primary evidence of what happened at Damascus. The three texts, Galatians 1:15–16, 1 Corinthians 9:1, 16 and 1 Corinthians 15:8–11, are not disinterested neutral descriptions of that event. In these contexts the apostle appeals to Damascus in the defense of his gospel, of his apostolic freedom, of his apostolic authority and of the resurrection of Jesus. Each reference is different and reflects the particular missionary situation.

> But when he who had set me apart before I was born, and had called me through his grace, was pleased to reveal his Son to me, in order that I might preach him among the Gentiles . . . (Gal 1:15–16).

> Am I not free? Am I not an apostle? Have I not seen Jesus Christ our Lord? (1 Cor 9:1).

> For if I preach the gospel, that gives me no ground for boasting. For necessity is laid upon me. Woe to me if I do not preach the gospel (1 Cor 9:16).

> Last of all, as to one untimely born, he appeared also to me. For I am the least of the apostles, unfit to be called an apostle, because I persecuted the church of God. But by the grace of God I am what I am, and his grace toward me was not in vain. On the contrary, I worked harder than any of them, though it was not I, but the grace of God which is in me. Whether then it was I or they, so we preached and so you believed (1 Cor 15:8–11).

In contrast to Luke's accounts, these texts are not in a story form. They do not recall the dialogue or describe the near circumstances, although some of these may be inferred. In fact, the apostle appears to be rather reticent about what actually transpired on that occasion. The important point which he makes here is not his personal conversion but rather the origin either of his gospel or of his apostolic calling. It is when these are questioned that he appeals to his founding experience at Damascus.

The most explicit account is that in Galatians 1. During Paul's absence from the community in Galatia, other, probably Jewish Christian missionaries, preached to the Galatian faithful, who were of Gentile origin, that they must accept the law of Moses and become circumcised. To Paul's mind this contravened his gospel that salvation is only through the saving deed of Jesus which is to be appropriated by faith in Jesus Christ. The new "gospel" probably called in question not so much the saving efficacy as the sufficiency of Christ. One way or the other, it challenged Paul's gospel and his apostolic authority to preach as he did. It is thus in defense of his gospel and of his apostolic authority that Paul here refers to Damascus.

In the context he affirms that he is "an apostle—not from men nor through man, but through Jesus Christ and God the Father, who raised him from the dead" (1:1). In other words, he received his call and authorization at Damascus.

Concerning the gospel he states that it "is not man's gospel. For I did not receive it from man nor was I taught it, but it came through a revelation of Jesus Christ" (1:11–12). He supports this by noting that, before his encounter at Damascus, he was an active persecutor of the Church, and that, after the encounter, he did not consult concerning the gospel with the pillars of the church in Jerusalem.

The revelation was the Father's disclosure of his Son to him, Paul, so that he might preach Christ to the Gentiles. God himself is thus the author of his gospel. The disclosure concerns Jesus as God's Son, who is the content of the gospel. Paul regards the revelation and call as a pure grace. Its only explanation is the pleasure of God and the will of God. The reference "he who set me apart before I was born" (1:15) is an allusion to Jeremiah 1:5 and Isaiah 49:1. It indicates that the apostle has reflected on and understood his call in the light of the Old Testament prophetic vocations.

The context of this passage thus indicates that Paul, up to the moment of revelation, persecuted the Church, and that the revelation and the call were something totally unexpected and sudden. The subsequent section mentions his proclamation in Syria and Cilicia and the report about him in the churches in Judea that "He

who once persecuted us is now preaching the faith he once tried
to destroy'' (1:23). The text and its context thus yield all the points of agreement
brought out by Munck. They go beyond Acts 9:22 and 26 in in-
sisting that the apostle had received the disclosure from God himself, that that act was a pure grace and the source of his gospel
and his commission. Paul insists on these realities because his
gospel and his authority were questioned in Galatia.
In comparison with this, 1 Corinthians 9 is not nearly as explicit. Here the apostle does not defend his gospel, but only his
right to preach his gospel free of charge, unlike some other com-
peting missionaries or even other apostles. He meets the objection
to his practice with three rhetorical questions: ''Am I not free? Am
I not an apostle? Have I not seen Jesus our Lord?'' The word
''Lord'' is Paul's usual title for Jesus. It expresses his present relationship with Jesus as his Lord. In vv. 16–19 the apostle then
discloses that the Lord has placed an obligation on him to proclaim
the gospel. We thus find here the three elements, the vision, the
gospel, and the apostolic commission.

In 1 Corinthians 15 Paul defends the reality of the future resurrection of the faithful against some in the community who were
denying it. He first reminds the faithful of the gospel which he
had preached to them. Yet here he does not derive this gospel from
his Damascus experience, as in Galatians 1, but rather points out
that he has handed down this gospel as he had received it, as the
common gospel in the churches. It is the gospel concerning the
death and the resurrection of Christ (vv. 3b–5). This quotation
ends with the affirmation ''and that he [Christ] appeared to Cephas and then to the twelve'' (v. 5) supporting the preceding statement ''that he was raised on the third day in accordance with the
scriptures.'' In subsequent verses (6–11) the apostle expands on
the appearances mentioned in v. 5 and gives a list of further appearances of the risen Christ, ending with the appearance to himself (v. 8). Against many scholars we hold that the primary

purpose in Paul's mentioning these appearances here, his own included, is to secure the reality of the resurrection of Jesus. The reason for this is plain: the resurrection of Jesus is the basis of hope concerning our resurrection. It is this hope, implied and guaranteed in the resurrection of Jesus, that the apostle defends in the entire chapter 15.

The above analysis of the context thus suggests that the statement in v. 8, "last of all, as to one untimely born, he appeared also to me," is to be regarded as another proof in support of the resurrection of Christ. The rest, vv. 9–11, is a parenthesis. Many scholars have lost sight of the parenthetical nature of these verses and have made it the main point. According to them, Paul is here defending his apostolic authority. But in the context of 1 Corinthians 15, this is only a side issue. However, the parenthesis does bring out that Paul had received his apostolic calling through the appearance to him of the risen Jesus, and that it was a pure and undeserved grace.

All these texts thus indicate that the apostle sees his gospel, vocation and authority rooted in the Damascus experience. They disclose that he is under the obligation to preach and that the content of his preaching is determined by the revelation at Damascus.

What Really Happened?

What did happen at Damascus? Scholarly literature on this subject is not unanimous. To some extent the answers differ only because exegetes are asking different questions and following diverse methodologies with implicit or explicit presuppositions. The problem is often whether the principles governing their investigations and the tools employed are appropriate and adequate to the subject matter, in this case Paul's experience at Damascus.

If we take the apostle at his word, he had a unique revelation of the Son of God, the risen Christ, which, he claims, is the sole source of his gospel and of his apostolic vocation. As a personal revelation, Paul's experience would seem to be outside the scope of an historical investigation. However, the apostle talked about it, used certain expressions to describe it, appealed to it in defense of his gospel and his authority. His entire life and thought show the impact of this experience. Examining these data some scholars have suggested that the matter is much more complex than Paul indicates. Some have questioned whether he in fact saw the risen Jesus, others whether he received on that occasion his gospel and his apostolic calling.

We find basically three kinds of explanations, historical, psychological and religious/supernatural. Some exegetes offer a natural and rational explanation, others admit the presence of the transcendent in the event.

Historians of the classical mold that follow the principles of D.F. Strauss exclude from their investigation all supernatural phenomena, since these are not subject to scientific control. They seek a meaningful explanation of an event within the relationship of natural causes and effects and in light of other historical events. A transcendent and wholly unique event is thus by this definition not subject to an historical analysis and explanation. It would appear, therefore, that the Damascus event as such falls outside the scope of an historical investigation, if we can believe Paul and Luke. But not so Paul's and Luke's descriptions of it. These texts, as human products, can be analyzed within their proper literary contexts and against the background of contemporary ideas. Hence scholars ask about possible later additions, modifications, explanations, conflations and the reasons for them. They try to establish the function and purpose of these references and the relationship of language and concepts to contemporary ideas and expressions. Their solutions, however, are not without some hypothetical reconstructions and must be tested against the texts.

Many scholars today hold that, from the historical perspective, some of the details and descriptions of the Damascus event as found in Acts can be accounted for as later additions and interpretations. It can be shown that Luke strongly reshaped whatever traditions he had at his disposal for his theological purposes which are apparent in Acts. Yet, as we have seen, the core of these accounts is in agreement with the affirmations of the apostle: He, persecutor of Christians, had a sudden and totally unexpected encounter with the risen Jesus at Damascus through which he became a believer and received his call as an apostle of the Gentiles.

But how do Paul's own statements fare under historical scrutiny? Scholars do not directly question the veracity and the sincerity of the apostle. However, some point out that he wrote many years after the event. Could it be that he conflated several things into one? Does not his interpretation reflect his later experiences and his mature theological thought (P. Gaechter, Rigaux)?[13]

Others have examined the function of Paul's references to the Damascus event. There is a growing consensus today that the apostle's purpose here was to legitimate his apostolic authority. U. Wilckens, who first worked out this interpretation, still holds that Paul truly encountered the risen Jesus. However, W. Marxsen and others dispute this. According to Marxsen,[14] the apostle had a ''vision'' of Jesus from which he *concluded* that he had seen the *risen* Jesus. This was an obvious conclusion in the apocalyptic milieu in which the resurrection of the dead was expected for the end time. There is thus no historical basis that Paul in fact saw the risen Jesus and that the resurrection of Jesus occurred. For Marxsen, the resurrection is a matter of faith, not of history. Paul's references to the Damascus event are therefore mere legitimations.

We cannot here take issue with Marxsen in detail; suffice it to point out that his historical procedure is governed by certain presuppositions not shared by historians in general. His argument from the apocalyptic view is inconclusive. The texts do not mention a ''bare'' vision but rather a revelation to Paul and a direct communication between (the risen) Jesus and Paul.

In the past, some scholars suggested a psychological explanation on the basis of Romans 7 and Gal 3:24, where the apostle apparently speaks of his past spiritual struggles. However, W. Kümmel and subsequent investigations have shown that these texts are not autobiographical. Paul's subsconscious motivation is simply no longer available to us or subject to scientific control. Moreover, as J.C. Beker has noted, "psychological reductionism cannot take the place of historical explanation."[15]

There are rational explanations of the experience of Paul that take account of religious factors. According to these, the apostle had a crisis of conscience or doubts concerning the validity of the law. These solutions as well lack biographical data and are, moreover, contradicted by Paul in Galatians 1, Philippians 3:4–6 and elsewhere. The apostle here describes himself as an enthusiastic follower and proponent of the law until his encounter at Damascus. "The most striking thing about Paul's conversion," according to Beker, "is its suddenness and unpreparedness. Both Acts and Paul agree on this."[16] Such a "crisis" would scarcely account for a profound and lasting change in the apostle's life in the wake of this experience.

Scholars who grant the transcendent nature of Paul's Damascus encounter explain it at times as a mystical experience like that mentioned in 2 Corinthians 12:1–4.[17] Here the vision was granted to "a man in Christ" who was "caught up in the third heaven" and "heard things that cannot be told, which man may not utter." Paul was not sure whether this man was "in the body or out of the body." However, according to Paul's description, the two experiences are distinct and different. 2 Corinthians 12 states that Paul was already deeply united with Christ ("a man in Christ"), that he fell into a trance and had a private disclosure not only of unspeakable realities but of things which may not be disclosed. In Galatians 1, however, we find that an opponent of Christ, a persecutor of Christians, received God's revelation of Jesus Christ and was called to preach him. Mystical experiences, as Rigaux observed,[18] are usually repeated phenomena granted to a person already deeply united with God in a life of contemplation.

Terms like trance, vision, and mystical experience convey only a part of what happened to Paul at Damascus. They focus more on the experience and perception of the person involved than on the act of revelation. The apostle himself uses terms like "revelation," "seeing the Lord" and "appearance."

Probably the closest parallels to Paul's experience at Damascus are accounts of prophetic vocations found in the Old Testament. Both the apostle and Luke see the Damascus event in that light. G. von Rad[19] has shown that these produced a profound and lasting change in the prophet, involving a call, a disclosure of God's word and the obligation to communicate it. Paul's experience differs from these in that, at Damascus, God revealed his Son to him, and that the persecutor became a believer. The call and the commission also distinguish Paul's encounter with the risen Christ from some of those mentioned in 1 Corinthians 15.

The Turning Point

Jeremias, Bornkamm and Beker emphasize that the Damascus experience was a turning point in Paul's life and made him reverse his former values. What were these values at stake for Paul?

Bornkamm and Beker maintain that Paul as a Pharisee objected above all to the Church's admitting Gentiles into its ranks without demanding that they be first circumcised. This was a breach of the law and threatened the constitution and the prerogatives of Israel. Paul was also convinced that Jesus was a pseudo-Messiah; the fact that God let him die on the cross was a telling proof of it. Yet this was probably not a decisive issue, for Judaism tolerated other messianic pretenders in the first two centuries A.D.

But at Damascus Paul realized that God in fact had raised Jesus from the dead. In that encounter—and this must be maintained—he came to know Jesus as the Son of God and as Lord affirmed through the resurrection. He understood for the first time that the crucifixion of Jesus was not a sign of God's displeasure toward the crucified one, but rather the unfathomable act of God's saving love in giving up his Son, as well as the self-giving love of Jesus. Jesus died for us by the will of God (Rom 5:6–10; 8:31–32; Gal 2:20). Paul realized that this is a new order of salvation open to all and a new aeon (Gal 4:4), replacing the old aeon and its law. It is only by embracing this offer of salvation that a person is set at rights with God.

Here is the beginning of Paul's faith and love of Christ. Here is also the basis of his gospel concerning God's Son and of his unique emphasis on Christ's death, resurrection and lordship.

In the light of this knowledge Paul reassessed his former values, such as the law and circumcision. These are no longer the way to God. He realized that a new access has been opened to God through Christ. What counts now is being with Christ, sharing in his death and in his resurrection. It is this that he appeals to in Galatians and Philippians. Justification and salvation are by faith in Christ, not through the law. He sees this as a consequence of God's sending his Son into the world.

Christ has thus become the supreme value for Paul. In comparison with this, his former values appeared as no values at all. The apostle brings this out most clearly in Philippians 3:3–9. Things that he once cherished, such as belonging to the people of Israel, being a Pharisee, being blameless under the law, he now regards as matters pertaining to the flesh. "But whatever gain I had, I counted as loss for the surpassing worth of knowing Jesus my Lord. . . . For his sake I have suffered the loss of all things, and count them as refuse, in order that I may gain Christ and be found in him. . . ."

It is Paul who gives us the profoundest reflections on the role of the law in God's plan of salvation (Rom 5:18–21; 7:1–25). He it was that also saw the connection between the law and the power of sin.

Even Paul's former understanding of the scriptures was affected by the Damascus experience. In 2 Corinthians 3:6–18 he confesses that the knowledge of Christ has made him see these writings in a new light, with an "unveiled face." The covenant, in which he used to glory, has become to him the "old covenant," a "dispensation of death," whose splendor "has come to have no splendor at all because of the splendor that surpasses it." He is now "beholding the glory of the Lord." God has qualified him as minister "of the new covenant, not written in code but in the Spirit." God has shone "in our hearts to give the light of the knowledge of the glory of God in the face of Christ" (2 Cor 4:6).

However, the deepest reason for the change in Paul was his knowledge of God's and Christ's love for him and for others. God's love was brought home to him in the revelation of the crucified Jesus as God's Son (Rom 5:6–10; 8:31–32; Gal 2:20). He was deeply moved by the enormity of God's love. The depth of this love for us can only be appreciated in the light of the unique relationship and love between the Father and the Son implied by the designation "Son of God." It was this act of God through his Son on our behalf that assured the apostle of God's undying and unchangeable love for us. He appeals to it and presents it as a firm basis of hope (Rom 5:6–10; 8:31–32).

It was the love of Christ for us, so manifestly clear in his death (Rom 5:6–8), that made everything else appear to Paul like rubbish and that set his heart on fire. We find in his writings an intense desire to be in Christ and with Christ. He wants to share in Christ's death and resurrection (Phil 3:10–11). He regards his apostolic efforts as a loving service to and glorification of Christ (Phil 1:20). In Galatians 2:20 he exclaims, "It is no longer I who live but Christ lives in me; and the life I now live in the flesh I live by faith in the Son of God, who loved me and gave himself for me.'' In Philippians 3:10–11 this desire becomes a burning wish to share Christ's sufferings—''That I . . . may share his sufferings, becoming like him in his death, that if possible I may attain the resurrection from the dead.'' The resurrection meant for Paul full fellowship and union with the Lord (1 Thess 4:13–18; 1 Cor 15; 2 Cor 5:1–10). In Philippians 1:20–23 this intense desire to be with Christ fully is anticipated through the expectation of being with Christ immediately upon death. ''My desire is to depart and be with Christ.'' And, for the apostle, to be found in Christ is to be found in God.

The Commission To Go to the Gentiles

In retrospect, at any rate, Paul claims that it was at Damascus that he had received his apostolic call. This is evident from all the passages we have examined above. In Galatians 1, moreover, he affirms that he was sent to the Gentiles. But was the call actually given at Damascus? And, if it was, how explicit was the commission to go to the Gentiles?

Some scholars suggest that the apostle, writing many years after the event at Damascus, simplified and condensed things. He attributed to that founding event a clarity of mission which, in fact, evolved only gradually in his consciousness through his meditating on it in light of Isaiah 49:1 and Jeremiah 1:5–8, through the course of later circumstances, and through subsequent visions. Gaechter holds that Paul received at Damascus only the revelation of the risen Jesus, whereas the call came to him at a later vision, perhaps in that mentioned in Acts 22:17–21. In contrast to this, L. Cerfaux, H. Schlier, Jeremias, Beker and most other scholars maintain that the apostle was given the call at the revelation at Damascus.

A middle ground between these solutions is suggested by B. Rigaux. According to him, ''the vision did not *per se* create Paul an Apostle,'' still less an apostle to the Gentiles, although he did receive some sort of call in a nuclear fashion at Damascus. "It contained the germ of a vocation that was to be revealed later." By this Rigaux means that it later became clear to Paul. What brought him to this conviction was the growth of the Church in Antioch (Gal 2:1–10), the first missionary endeavors, his own reflections upon God's action in light of the Old Testament (Gal 1:12–16) and the mounting polemics (1 Cor 11:23; 15:2–11). This gradual development is also reflected in Luke's accounts in Acts.[20]

This brings us to the experience of Paul mentioned in Acts 22:17–21. We find this account embedded in Luke's second description of Paul's Damascus experience. To his Jewish audience in Jerusalem Paul tells that, in a trance, as he was praying in the temple, the Lord told him: "Make haste and get quickly out of Jerusalem, because they will not accept your testimony about me." At the end, the apostle hears the words; "Depart; for I will send you far away to the Gentiles." Paul here recounts both the general commission he had received at Damascus and a later, more explicit instruction. The new direction is thus the Lord's will. Luke indicates that this turn of direction occurred when the apostle returned to Jerusalem from his journey to Damascus, hence relatively soon after the vision at Damascus.

How does this directive relate to Paul's commission at Damascus? We find that the three accounts in Acts are not identical, but rather complementary. According to Acts 9:6 Paul himself was not given a mission instruction by the Lord. That is found in the Lord's explanation to Ananias. The reader thus knows of God's choice of and design for Paul. In the second account, Acts 22, Ananias in fact informs Paul of this. According to the third account, Acts 26, the Lord himself tells Paul, "Rise and stand on your feet; for I have appeared to you for this purpose, to appoint you to serve and to bear witness to the things in which you have

seen me and to those in which I will appear to you, delivering you from the people and from the Gentiles—to whom I send you to open their eyes . . ." (vv. 16–18).
Luke thus affirms the commission at Damascus as well as the instruction at Jerusalem. He does not play one against the other. In Acts 22 he relates the later directive to the founding vision, and in Acts 26 he makes room in the commission at Damascus for the later instructions. The directive in Jerusalem is, in Luke's view, one of the many specific commands the apostle received in the course of his carrying out the original commission (see 13:1–3; 16:6, 7, 9–10). This is in agreement with the general theme in Acts that the mission of the early Church continued to be guided by the Spirit and by the risen Lord.

The accounts in Acts thus only slightly support the contention of Rigaux that Paul received his call at Damascus simply in a nuclear fashion and that the specific direction of his mission became clear to him later on. The apostle's own statements and recollections do not mirror such a development of consciousness. The opinion of Gaechter that Paul actually received the call in Jerusalem has no support in Acts, still less in Pauline epistles.

The Impact on Paul's Gospel and Theology

Paul's call was not preceded by a period of association with and following of the earthly Jesus. As Beker points out, Paul did not listen, as other apostles did, to the master's talk and was not an eyewitness with them to the resurrection appearances. Rather, he came to know Jesus only in the flash of the end-time revelation as the Christ, the Lord and the Son of God with a unique and dominant role in God's plan of salvation.[21] Both the apostle's own accounts as well as those in Acts agree with this.

A historian and exegete cannot deny *a priori* the possibility of this revelation or that it occurred. But a historian can examine to what extent the later thought of the apostle reflects this unique experience, check for a possible development, and determine the presence and the extent of other influences on the theology of Paul.

As we have seen above, Marxsen dismisses the aspect of revelation in Paul's Damascus experience, and other scholars have suggested certain rational explanations for that experience. Yet none of them account adequately for the unique aspects of Paul's theology and for the subsequent life of the apostle.

Most scholars (Jeremias, Beker, Bornkamm, Cerfaux, Rigaux, Fitzmyer) acknowledge that the revelation at Damascus is the mainspring of Paul's gospel even as they admit other influences on it, including the early Church's tradition. According to Beker, Paul's conversion and call have been taken into this revelation and play a relatively minor role in the apostle's gospel. His gospel is not pious retelling of his personal conversion. It is rather a proclamation of ''the new state of affairs that God has initiated in Christ, one that concerns nations and creation. . . . Christ is the object and the content of the gospel.''[22]

According to Galations 1:16, Paul received at Damascus a revelation of God's Son that he may preach him among the Gentiles. His gospel is thus about God's Son. This theme is central to him, as it is elsewhere in the New Testament. As 1 Corinthians 15 indicates, the proclamation of the apostle is about the death, the resurrection and the lordship (including the parousia) of Christ and agrees with the Church's proclamation. But what is peculiar to his way of proclaiming is the high road of transmission, as opposed to the low road found in the four gospels. We find little in Paul about the sayings and the deeds of the earthly Jesus, with the exception of the eucharistic passage, 1 Corinthians 11:23 and a few fragmentary references to the sayings of the Lord. Everything is scen in the light of the consummation. This, scholars agree, is the result of Paul's peculiar encounter with the risen Jesus at Damascus. The universality of salvation, the emphasis on the new creation, on faith, on the end of the law is another side of his gospel corresponding to the destination, the Gentiles.

Not only the apostle's gospel in the narrower sense, but his entire thought and theology bear the imprint of Damascus. This experience alone, according to Jeremias, explains Paul's sudden break with his past, his profound change of values and his unique apostolic consciousness reflected in his writings. Jeremias roots the following aspects of Pauline theology in Damascus: (1) Paul's personal fellowship and union with Christ; (2) his profound understanding of the cross; (3) his awareness of the all-powerful grace of God; (4) the realization that God's choice precedes all human effort; (5) the horror of sin; (6) his radical rejection of the law; (7) the resurrection of Christ as the basis of the resurrection of the faithful; (8) the identification of the Lord with the Church.[23] But to what extent are these characteristics of Pauline theology rooted in the revelation at Damascus? Were they fully revealed to Paul on that occasion or only in a nuclear fashion? Docs his theology show a development?

Rigaux, who admits the reality of the Damascus revelation, chides E.B. Allo, H. Dieckmann and Y. Zapelena for too lightly regarding the historical development and the textual evidence. According to him, the apostle did not receive at Damascus the "necessary knowledge to conquer the entire world." With Gaechter he cautions that such a position "incurs the risk of positing a twofold foundation of Christianity: An institutional foundation by the twelve and a charismatic foundation by Paul."[24]

Rigaux voices here a concern which is heard more frequently among Catholic than among Protestant exegetes. Whereas many Protestant scholars tend to see the entire New Testament in the light of Pauline theology, Rigaux, Ph.H. Menoud and Cerfaux emphasize the unity of the New Testament and subsume Paul's theology to it. They point out that the apostle appealed also to traditions of the Church, was conscious of the unity among all believers, and sought the approval of "men in authority" in Jerusalem (Gal 2:1–10). The basis of this, according to Cerfaux, is the unity of the risen Christ: the various traditions "merged into the same faith and in the same notion of a living and teaching community."[25]

There is some validity in Rigaux's caution. We must not read back into Paul's Damascus experience all the explicit theological ideas found in his writings. Most scholars would hold that Pauline theology shows signs of development. Instances of this would be the later downplaying of the parousia expectation, shift to the present union with Christ, switch to the union with Christ immediately upon one's death, focus on justification by faith, etc. The apostle did not become instantly equipped with the theology that we find in his letters written some twenty years after the Damascus revelation. Some of it, at least, is the fruit of his later reflections occasioned by circumstances, by missionary needs, and by other traditions.

On the other hand, there is evidence that Paul integrated his later experiences and reflections with the revelation at Damascus. According to Fitzmyer, what the apostle inherited from his Hellenistic and Jewish backgrounds, what he borrowed from tradition, and what he arrived at through his missionary experience, is all "uniquely transformed by his knowledge of Christ which he received at Damascus. There is an inner unity of mission and theology in Paul explained only by his Damascus experience."[26]

2
The Resurrection of Christ

At Damascus, as we have seen, Paul encountered the risen Jesus and came to know the saving significance of Christ's death and resurrection. The letters of the apostle indicate that he is a profound theologian of the resurrection. We ask here: What does Paul say about the resurrection of Christ? How do exegetes interpret these statements of the apostle?

We shall limit our discussion to certain opinions in the recent past. But first let us try to see what Paul himself says on this topic.

The Resurrection Appearances and the Resurrection of Jesus

The key text dealing with this issue is 1 Corinthians 15:3–11. In vv. 3–8 the apostle states,

> I delivered to you as of first importance what I also received, 3b that Christ died for our sins in accordance with the scriptures, 4 that he was buried, that he was raised on the third day in accordance with the scriptures, 5 that he appeared to Cephas, then to the twelve. 6 Then he appeared to more than five hundred brethren at one time, most of whom are still alive, though some have fallen asleep. 7 Then he appeared to

James, then to all the apostles. 8 Last of all, as to one untimely born, he appeared also to me.

Paul then goes on to talk about his own choice by grace as an apostle and about his proclamation of this Easter message (vv. 9–11).

Most scholars agree that vv. 3b–5 came from a pre-Pauline
Church tradition. Many would agree that vv. 6–8 were probably
appended by Paul and that they contain a tradition or information
known to him.[1] We regard them as an expansion of v. 5. Their
role and function must be seen in the context of chapter 15 which
deals with the resurrection of the dead, or, more precisely, with
the future resurrection of the faithful.

In this chapter the apostle tries to correct an opinion which
arose among some Christians in Corinth that there is no (future)
resurrection of the dead (see v. 12). There is a great deal of scholarly discussion about the exact nature of this view, Paul's understanding of it and his reaction to it. Some suggest a gnostic
doctrine, others a syncretistic tendency, others again a Hellenistic
philosophical disparagement of the body, still others an enthusiastic overemphasis on the present spiritual experience of salvation. We need not concern ourselves here with these opinions and
reconstructions. It is enough to say that the apostle understood the
view to involve an interpretation of Christian existence in which
the ultimate completion did not involve the resurrection of the
dead as he had preached it.

To Paul's mind this opinion undermined his gospel and en-
dangered the salvation of the faithful. In vv. 1–2 he therefore reminds the Corinthians of the gospel he has preached and of its
salvific importance. In the section that follows, vv. 12–19, he
then argues that to deny the (future) resurrection is also to deny
Christ's resurrection and consequently to empty the content and
the saving power of faith. The resurrection of Christ embraces the
resurrection of the faithful in such a way that to deny one is to
deny the other. In v. 20 he again affirms the resurrection of Christ

and then talks about the time of the resurrection of the faithful, its mode and its meaning for salvation.

With this in mind let us now return to vv. 3b–8. To meet this inherent danger to salvation, the apostle quotes in vv. 3b–5 a summary of his gospel and of the gospel proclaimed by the Church. It concerns the saving death of Christ and his resurrection. The last statement, "and that he appeared to Cephas, then to the twelve" (v. 5) supports the preceding sentence that Christ "was raised on the third day in accordance with the scriptures." Since Paul in this chapter presents Christ's resurrection as the basis of the future resurrection, he affirms it here by adding to v. 5 a list of further appearances of the risen Christ, including at the end the appearance of Christ to Paul himself (vv. 6–8a). The apostle thereby presents the resurrection of Christ as a fact attested to by the subsequent resurrection appearances. This is apparent from his own remark in v. 6, "some of them are still alive, though some have fallen asleep," i.e. some of the five hundred brethren are still alive and can verify that Christ appeared to them. For Paul, the fact of Christ's appearances testifies to the fact of his resurrection.

Difficulties with Paul's Argumentation

The apostle's argumentation here caused problems to some exegetes in the twentieth century. Some find it faulty for theological reasons (R. Bultmann), others suggest that he really did not intend to give here a proof of the resurrection of Christ (K. Barth). These difficulties stem from certain presuppositions about the resurrection and faith which apparently are not shared by Paul. Bultmann, for example, concedes that the apostle is here proving the fact of the resurrection of Christ. But, according to him, such argumentation is wrong. Paul should not be proving by historical means a reality which pertains to faith.[2] Besides, for Bultmann, the resurrection of Christ means something quite different from what it meant to Paul. But we shall say more about this later.

Barth is also uncomfortable with this argumentation in 1 Corinthians 15:5–8. He, however, suggests that Paul listed here the
resurrection appearances in order to bring out the agreement of his
gospel with that of the Church.[3] But this solution scarcely reflects
the flow of the apostle's argumentation. The agreement with the
Church is already unmistakably stated in v. 3a, and the apostle's
own parenthetical comment inserted into the list itself in v. 6b
clearly brings out his intention, which is to point to the self-dis-
closures of the risen Jesus as evidence that he was raised from the
dead. This is the thrust of Paul's argument in vv. 1–20 (see esp.
vv. 14 and 20).

Appearances as Legitimations

A more recent interpretation of the resurrection appearances
is offered by Wilckens. A more radical form of it is presented by
Marxsen and Pesch. All of them attempt to provide historical
meaning to references to the resurrection appearances in the original context.

Wilckens acknowledges that the apostle used the list of the
resurrection appearances as evidence of Jesus' resurrection. However, according to him, this is only one of the functions of the
appearances. The other is to legitimate his authority and his call,
in the community. Paul makes references to the appearances in
this sense in 1 Corinthians 9:1, 15:8–11 and Galatians 1:12, 15.
Since the appearance of the risen Christ to him involved Paul's
personal call to be the apostle of the Gentiles, he had to affirm it
on several occasions by recalling that experience. This suggests
that others, mentioned by him in 1 Corinthians 15:5–7, also appealed to the appearances of the risen Jesus for the same reason.
They, as well, claimed thereby not only to be witnesses to Jesus'
resurrection, but also to have received special authority. The appearances, witnessing to Jesus' resurrection, legitimations, and

the mission to proclaim the risen Christ go together in this understanding of the resurrection appearances.[4]

We would agree that the references to the resurrection appearance of Jesus to the apostle have this twofold function, but we would disagree that the second function is apparent in 1 Corinthians 15:5–11. Wilckens finds evidence of this in vv. 8–11. However, vv. 8b–11, which follow the apostle's reference to his own encounter with the risen Christ, are a parenthesis. The words "to one untimely born," "the least of the apostles," and "unfit to be called an apostle" are scarcely self-legitimations. For his own right and duty to preach as he did, Paul appeals here to "the grace of God" which *is with him*. His final words, "whether then it is I or they, so we preach and so we believe," relativize the person and the authority of the proclaimer, the apostle included. What is important is this particular gospel and its reception by faith. Paul does not here legitimate his apostolic authority and the right to preach, but rather the preaching of Jesus' resurrection, either by himself or by others. This indicates that the structure of Pauline references to the resurrection of Jesus varies and that it is hazardous to project one of its functions onto the earlier, non-Pauline references.

There are, moreover, indications that neither the apostle nor the (Hellenistic) tradition before him understood all these references as legitimations. The way Paul used them is clear from v. 6. For the earlier tradition, it is difficult to see what authority the five hundred brethren claimed to have because of the appearance of the risen Jesus to them. The gospel traditions mention other appearances which cannot be interpreted as legitimations.

In contrast to Wilckens, who maintains a twofold function of the references to the resurrection appearances, Pesch, a Catholic, regards them as mere legitimations. His intention is to give an historical and rational explanation of the rise of faith. According to him, that faith rose through the disciples' association with the earthly Jesus and continued uninterrupted after the Easter events.

The resurrection appearances are not historical and hence do not witness to the resurrection of Jesus. The talk about the resurrection of Jesus is a way of expressing the end-time meaning, mission and authority of Jesus. In view of Jesus' death on the cross, the language of resurrection expresses also God's legitimation of the crucified, i.e., God's approval.[5]

Pesch's solution comes close to Marxsen's and probably depends on it.[6] We have already seen that Marxsen, in the case of Paul, admits that the apostle had a real vision of Jesus from which he deduced that Jesus rose from the dead. From the historical perspective of today and from the twentieth-century anthropology, that vision, which did not contain any extra revelation, does not warrant such a conclusion. It is, moreover, not necessary for faith. The same holds for other appearances of Jesus after Easter which are mentioned in 1 Corinthians 15:5–7.

According to Marxsen, an historian can only say that the individuals and the groups mentioned in 1 Corinthians 15:5–7 claimed that "something happened to them which they described as seeing Jesus."[7] They interpreted this happening in two directions, backward and forward.

In answer to the question "How could this vision of Jesus ever have come about?"[8] they deduced that he was raised from the dead. This was their reflection on the appearance, not factual evidence, and looks backward. It is a reasoning in faith suggested to them by their Jewish anthropology that incorporated the hope in the resurrection in the end-time.

The other, forward-directed interpretation, deals with the function of the appearance. This is not a reflection of the witnesses, as is the previous one, but a direct product of the encounter. The appearance brought about a commission: the witnesses are to set up a community and bring into being functions within the community. The content of the commission is to continue the mission of Jesus.

According to this view the purpose of Jesus is to be sustained through the preaching of his witnesses. Marxsen refers to Bultmann's summation of this as: "Jesus rose into the kerygma." He agrees with Bultmann's meaning, but objects to the term "rose." According to him the sentence should read: "Jesus is alive in the kerygma." The proclamation by the witnesses is "the continuing occurrence of the *kerygma of Jesus*."[9] According to Marxsen, the believer today who says, "he is the Risen One because he (identical with the earthly Jesus) still *comes* today with the same (old) claim," does not need the concept of the "Risen One."[10] The language of the resurrection is not necessary or possible for us today to express this reality or the hope in the future.

The affirmation of the resurrection of Jesus is, accordingly, not a fact immediately evident in Jesus' appearances, but a statement and a supposition of faith which can also be expressed otherwise. Marxsen admits that all the early witnesses believed this to be true, but this does not mean that believers in the twentieth century should also believe it. The former expressed their faith within the horizon of Jewish anthropology. If Greeks had had a similar appearance of Jesus, they would have expressed it differently, i.e., within their anthropology. At any rate, the anthropology of today forbids the earliest interpretation.

Both Marxsen and Pesch tried to give a purely "historical" explanation of the rise of Easter faith. Their solutions differ, however. According to Marxsen, the disciples concluded from the appearances, as they were expected to in the apocalyptic horizon, that Jesus rose from the dead, etc. In the opinion of Pesch, the appearances did not happen, i.e., they are not verified historically. Hence the disciples did not conclude to the resurrection of Jesus. They merely used the language of resurrection to express the reality of faith which they had had ever since their encounter with the earthly Jesus and the eschatological significance of Jesus. Pesch's solution does not explain the rise of Easter faith in Paul who did not meet the earthly Jesus and did not believe prior to the Damascus encounter.

Wilckens[11] objects that Marxsen's explanation does not make historically plausible how the disciples, after the crucifixion of Jesus, could still continue to believe in the cause of Jesus as divinely approved. The Jewish milieu would make this even more difficult: Did not the form of Jesus' death, his death on the cross, indicate God's disapproval of Jesus? After all, the law cursed the crucified. According to Wilckens, the only reason why the disciples cleared this hurdle is that Jesus revealed himself to them in the end-time glory. It was this that signified to the witnesses God's approval of Jesus.

We have several difficulties with Marxsen's argumentation. We shall mention here only a few of them. Marxsen strips the appearance to the occurrence of a bare vision devoid of any (special) revelation. This, however, does not hold for all the appearances of Jesus. The apostle speaks of God's revelation of his Son to him, Paul, in which he received the call to preach Jesus to the Gentiles. This appearance, accordingly, brought about in Paul a knowledge of the action of God in this revelation, of Jesus as God's Son, and of the call to preach Christ among the Gentiles. The gospel accounts also describe certain appearances as revelations in word and gesture, some of them disclosing the identity of Jesus, others conveying the commission.

Admittedly, this is not verifiable by the tools of history which, by definition, are not meant to and cannot deal with occurrences of supernatural interventions in human affairs. However, to deny on that ground the fact or the possibility of this occurrence and to imperiously relegate affirmations about it to the realm of faith is itself illegitimate by the rules of historical procedures so defined. It rests on the assumption that the science of history can give an adequate explanation of every fact, and that what history cannot explain has no claim to be regarded as a fact.

If the appearance to Paul did not contain any revelation at all, how then did he recognize, in what he saw, Jesus whom he had never met? How could he, solely on the basis of this "experience of seeing'' and of this sight whose meaning was yet to be determined, have overcome his former opposition to the crucified and to the claim of Christians that Jesus had been raised from the dead? And how could he understand that this vision called him personally to be an apostle of the Gentiles? Wilckens raises against Marxsen similar questions concerning other appearances mentioned in 1 Corinthians 15:5–7.

Another weakness in Marxsen's historical explanation is that he wholly disregarded the basic problem for faith that the death of Jesus had caused in that historical environment. This is also a weakness of Pesch's historical analysis. Wilckens[12] has brought out that, since the law cursed the one who hangs on a tree, the crucifixion of Jesus would have been interpreted in that milieu as God's disapproval of the crucified and of his cause. A mere vision of Jesus after his death would scarcely be enough to dispel this doubt. Even the realization that Jesus was raised by God would not suffice, for it was held then that good and bad would both be raised by God and that the final judgment alone would determine God's approval. Only after this judgment would God's decision be known, when the bad would go to condemnation and those approved by God to glory.

Thus the statement ''Jesus rose from the dead'' does not by itself convey what Marxsen says it did, i.e., that the cause of Jesus goes on, and this with God's approval. What is still missing, according to Wilckens, is the *sign* of God's approval of Jesus and of his message and claim. That, he holds, was given to the witnesses by the revelation of Jesus in the end-time glory.[13]

In connection with this Wilckens brings out an important point: The faith of the early witnesses included belief in the lordship of the risen Jesus. How could this idea, so essential to Christian faith, have come about? It is a post-Easter understanding and cannot be derived from the disciples' relationship with Jesus before his death. At any rate, Marxsen would not argue that it did derive from that source. If the disciples were only certain *that* they saw Jesus, how did they come to believe that he is Lord?

This brings up the question of the adequacy of Bultmann's reinterpretation of the resurrection faith and of Marxsen's variation of that, but we need not go into that here.

3
The Meaning of Christ's Resurrection

We have brought out that, in 1 Corinthians 15:1–11, Paul restates his gospel of the death and resurrection of Christ. His real intention in this chapter, however, is to affirm the future resurrection of the dead. It is in this context that he draws out the meaning of Christ's resurrection. He relates it to the future resurrection of the faithful, to the present appropriation through faith, to the present lordship of the risen Christ, and to the completion of that lordship at the end-time coming of Christ.

The Resurrection of the Faithful as Implication of Christ's Resurrection

Having reaffirmed the resurrection of Christ in 1 Corinthians 15:1–11, the apostle, in the section that follows, argues about the reality of the (future) resurrection.

Now if Christ is preached as raised from the dead, how can some of you say that there is no resurrection of the dead? 13 But if there is no resurrection of the dead, then Christ has not been raised; 14 if Christ has not been raised, then our preaching is in vain and your faith is in vain. . . . 18 Then those who have fallen asleep in Christ have perished. 19 If for this life only we have hoped in Christ, we are of all men most to be pitied.

Paul then goes on to say,

But in fact Christ has been raised from the dead, the first fruits of those who have fallen asleep. 21 For as by a man came death, by a man has come the resurrection of the dead. 22 For as in Adam all die, so also in Christ shall all be made alive.

These texts clearly link the resurrection of Christ with the general resurrection of the dead. In vv. 12–19 the argument is negative, drawing out the consequence: the denial of the resurrection means the denial of Christ's resurrection with dire results for faith and salvation.

This is more than the merely logical conclusion from the universal to the particular, suggested by some scholars. As vv. 20–22 indicate, Paul's thought rests on the fundamental conviction and understanding that the resurrection of Christ involves the resurrection of all. It is directed toward all and it represents the beginning of the resurrection of all. Just as Adam's death is the root of the death of all, so Christ's resurrection is the root of life for all. It is thus not a single, isolated event in the past or an exception, but rather the new order of life for everybody. Christ is "the first fruits of those who have fallen asleep."

This is a fundamental affirmation of the apostle and the basis of his argument here. In this respect his perspective differs from the view held in Jewish apocalyptic. It is sometimes also suggested that, in Jewish apocalyptic, the eschatological nature of anyone's resurrection means, by itself and automatically, the beginning of the end-time resurrection. Yet we do not find this view in Jewish apocalyptic, nor is this how Paul argues here.

Neither does the apostle's view rest exclusively on the

Adam-Christ typology or on the special all-inclusive nature of Christ. He makes use of this comparison only to bring out the universal function of Christ's resurrection by the will of God. In v. 34 he indicates that his understanding of the resurrection derives from the knowledge of God, and in vv. 23–28 he speaks about God's endowment of the risen Christ with universal lordship. The purpose of this lordship is to annihilate death and its allies through the risen Christ's activity in the present and through his action in the final resurrection of the dead.

Thus, according to Paul, the resurrection of Christ and the general resurrection, though not fused, go together. The latter is the purpose and the completion of the former, not automatically, but by the will of God and through the activity of the risen Christ. In vv. 23–28 the apostle limits the general resurrection to the faithful, i.e., to those who belong to Christ. This brings us to the saving significance of Christ's resurrection and of the resurrection of the faithful.

Resurrection as a Salvific Event

If we examine again the credal formula in 1 Corinthians 15:3b–5, we discover that it attributes to Christ's death a saving significance: he died "for our sins." However, we do not find in the formula a comparable phrase drawing out the meaning of Christ's resurrection. Is the latter then without a salvific value?

Let us distinguish between the formula and the statements of Paul. We need not concern ourselves here with the former. If, however, we look at chapter 15, i.e., at what the apostle himself states, we discover that the entire chapter is about the saving significance of Christ's resurrection.

In Christ's resurrection, according to Paul, death lost its dominion over Christ and over human beings (vv. 20–22, 54–57). Not only did Christ rise never to die again (see Rom 6:9; cf. Acts 13:34), but in him all shall be made alive, i.e., all will share in his kind of life that is no longer subject to death, and in his victory over death (vv. 48–55). Christ is "the first fruits of those who have fallen asleep" (v. 20). Hence, just as he died "for us," so, also, he was raised for us, i.e., to bring about our resurrection. All this is seen as God's action on our behalf and as part of God's plan.

This means that the resurrection of Christ, seen in its root meaning, is in itself a saving event, for in it the hold of death over mankind has been broken. Death is seen here not merely as a natural event, but in its root meaning as a profound alienation between mankind and God due to the intrusion of sin into the world. The resurrection in the end-time will be the extension of Christ's resurrection to those who belong to him and a sharing in it (vv. 23–49). Hence it, as well, is regarded as a saving event, the end of man's alienation from God. In this respect the apostle's view of the future completion again differs from that in Jewish apocalyptic, where the resurrection is a "neutral" event that makes possible the final judgment and the consequent damnation or glorification (see Dan 12:2).

The saving significance of Christ's resurrection and of the end-time resurrection is expressed also by means of the lordship of the risen Christ. Through his resurrection Christ became Lord, endowed with power (Rom 1:4; Phil 2:9–11). God "has put all things in subjection under his feet" (1 Cor 15:27). According to vv. 23–28, the risen Christ is now actively promulgating and bringing to bear his power against death and related forces in the world and will totally annihilate these at his end-time coming through the resurrection and transformation (vv. 51–55). The resurrection in the end-time thus belongs to the completion of the risen Christ's lordship and to his salvific role according to which he is to bring all into the kingdom of God (v. 28).

Paul therefore regards the resurrection of Christ or the risen Christ as a life-giving power. "The last Adam became a life-giving spirit" (v. 45). In Philippians 3:10 he states that his one desire is to "know him [Christ] and the power of his resurrection." According to Philippians 3:21, the Lord "will change our mortal body . . . by the power which enables him even to subject all things to himself."

It follows that, for the apostle, salvation involves more than the forgiveness of sins. It includes the resurrection. The latter, however, is again more than mere immortality of the soul or of the resurrected body. It embraces a transformation of the body, eternal life in union, conformity and fellowship with the risen Christ, and a sharing in the glory of Christ's resurrection (v. 49). Salvation, according to Paul, is fused with the resurrection.

The way of salvation, in the wake of Easter, leads through the present experience of the saving reality. Paul describes it as the reign of Christ (vv. 24–25). The faithful are elsewhere referred to as "those who are being saved" (1 Cor 1:18). They have been redeemed from the power of sin (Rom 6:6–11), justified (Rom 5:1–2), reconciled with God (Rom 5:1–2), and given the Spirit of the risen Christ (Rom 8:9–11). The future resurrection presupposes this present and preliminary sharing in salvation. According to 1 Corinthians 15:23, (only) "those who belong to him [Christ]" will be raised from the dead.

We note that in 1 Corinthians 15 the apostle does not stress the present experience of salvation, probably because that has been emphasized by some in the community at the expense of the final salvation through the resurrection from the dead. In fact, he stresses the "not yet" of salvation. The ultimate completion, the kingdom of God, according to him, calls for the transformation (1 Cor 15:50–55). His own yearning is to be fully with Christ.

However, in other contexts, Paul can emphasize also the present experience of salvation: the union with Christ, the sharing in Christ's death and life, the gift of the Spirit, the adoption as sons and daughters through Christ, etc.

The resurrection of Christ is thus a basis of hope. What happened to Christ will happen also to those who belong to him. Just as God has raised Christ from the dead, so, also, he will raise the faithful from the dead. More fundamentally, the resurrection of Christ is a basis of hope as a manifestation of the love, the power and the faithfulness of God. It gives us the knowledge of God and of his plan for us through Christ. This aspect of hope has not yet been sufficiently elucidated by scholars.

The Subject, the Time, and the Mode of the Resurrection

Who is the *subject* of this hope? Who qualifies for the attainment of this glorious completion? We have seen that the apostle at first affirms that Christ was raised to bring life to all: "For as in Adam all die, so in Christ shall all be made alive" (1 Cor 15:22). However, in the next verse he restricts this expectation to "those who belong to Christ" (v. 23). Elsewhere Paul assumes that the actual solidarity with the risen Christ in the end-time resurrection extends only to those who are in solidarity with Christ in the present. It includes those who have been justified (Rom 5:1–10), who are "in Christ" (Rom 6:11), in whom Christ lives (Gal 2:20), etc. This is commonly admitted by scholars. As we have seen, in these passages, the present union with Christ is regarded as the necessary step toward the attainment of the promise of the ultimate union with Christ.

We find therefore at times in these contexts a demand for an interior commitment, which involves faith, love and hope. According to Romans 6:6–11 Christian existence calls for dying to the old self. Galatians 5:16–24 demands that the faithful follow the guidance of the Spirit. Hence the real subject of the resurrection hope is a committed believer.

In Romans 8:19–23, however, the apostle states that the entire creation will, in some way, share in the ultimate glory of the "sons of God." Creation will then itself be liberated from the oppressive condition in which it finds itself ever since the fall of Adam. This theme is also suggested in 1 Corinthians 15:24–28.

The *time* of the general resurrection is the end-time. Paul emphasizes this in 1 Corinthians 15. It coincides with the coming of the Lord. In vv. 23–28 the apostle distinguished between two stages of the resurrection, that of Christ, which is the root and the promise, and that of those who belong to Christ in the present.

Throughout his letters, the apostle retains the conviction that the resurrection of the dead and the coming of the Lord will take place in the end-time. Recent exegetical investigators (H.A. Wilcke, P. Hoffman)[1] have brought out that Paul did not expect a millennial reign between the parousia of Christ and the end-time kingdom of God. Neither did he speak about the interim existence between one's death and the general resurrection of the dead.

There are two texts, however, which are not easily integrated into this perspective, 2 Corinthians 5:1–10 and Philippians 1:23. In both of them the apostle expresses his ultimate hope beyond his own death. Many scholars hold that Paul here shifted his vision of the ultimate fulfillment from the end-time resurrection to the moment of one's death. As the turning point in his thinking, they mention his confrontation with death referred to in 2 Corinthians 1:8–11.

Yet the conclusion which the apostle draws in 2 Corinthians 1:10 is not that he is likely to die before the Lord's coming, but a renewed hope that God will continue to rescue him: "He [God] delivered us from so deadly a peril, and he will deliver us; on him we have set our hope that he will deliver us again." Nothing in the text indicates that this particular experience was a turning point in Paul's vision of hope. As 2 Corinthians 11:23–29 and other texts show, the apostle had faced death on many occasions.

P. Hoffmann[2] has shown that, in 2 Corinthians 5:1–10, Paul describes the fulfillment beyond death, i.e., the acquisition of an immortal and heavenly body, in opposition to a view that the ultimate completion will be a life outside this body. According to Hoffmann, the text must be read in light of 2 Corinthians 4:14, where the apostle expresses his belief "that he who raised the

Lord Jesus will raise us also with Jesus and bring us with you into his presence.''

However, in Philippians 1:21–23, where he is again facing death, Paul does express a desire to die and so be with the Lord. As Hoffmann[3] has observed, the text does not indicate that this life with Christ beyond death is an incomplete existence. The apostle does not here relate this fulfillment to the expectation of the end-time resurrection, yet in this epistle the hope in the final resurrection and in the Lord's coming is clearly maintained (1:6, 10–11; 3:20–21; 4:5). Hoffmann suggests that Paul had been holding both views and that the fulfillment at death is not a shift in his perspective of the future fulfillment. The apostle held before, during and after his writing Philippians that the completion would take place through the resurrection at the coming of Christ in the end-time.

The *mode* of the resurrection is indicated with the word ''transformation,'' emphasized by Paul in 1 Corinthians 15:35–55. In vv. 51–52 he informs the Corinthians: ''I tell you a mystery. We shall not all sleep, but we shall all be changed. . . . The dead will be raised imperishable, and we shall be changed.'' The apostle does not here affirm the imperishability of a spiritual existence, but that the whole human existence in the transformed body is imperishable. He stresses that it will be a *transformed* bodily existence, for ''flesh and blood'' cannot inherit the kingdom of God (v. 50).

Paul thus reassures the Corinthians that the resurrection will not be a return to this body which is weak, ignoble and corruptible. Yet he insists on the resurrection/transformation of *the body*. He uses words like ''spiritual,'' ''powerful,'' ''glorious,'' ''heavenly,'' ''incorruptible'' and ''immortal'' to describe the newness and the otherness of the end-time fulfillment in the body (vv. 42–54).

The emphasis here is on the transformation, *not* on the creation out of nothing as some scholars maintain. To illustrate the continuity, Paul employs the comparison of seed which dies in the earth and from which rises a plant (vv. 35–37). The agent of the resurrection is either God, or the Spirit, or the risen Lord, depending on the context. What the apostle teaches about the resurrection of Christians is thus a projection of what he knows of the resurrection of Christ. For him, Christ is the pattern for the rest. Just as the faithful share in the death of Christ, so, also, they will share in his resurrection (2 Cor 4:14; Rom 6:1–11).

The Resurrection, the Lordship, and the Coming of Christ

Paul, as we have seen, agrees with the view of the early Church that through the resurrection Jesus became Lord (Rom 1:3–4; Phil 2:6–11). Alluding to Psalm 8:6 he states in 1 Corinthians 15:27 that "God has put all things in subjection under his feet." On the basis of Psalm 110:1 he affirms that Christ must reign until he has put all things under his feet. Romans 1:3–4 and Philippians 2:6–11 imply that the resurrection of Christ was the beginning of his reign, of his messianic function entrusted to him by the Father.

As 1 Corinthians 15:23–28 indicates, Christ's reign is not a peaceful possession of power and glory in the heavenly realm, but rather a present and active enforcement of his rule in the cosmos. Christ is presented here as a warrior: he is now subjugating forces hostile to God and to the faithful, hence the saving action on behalf of the faithful continues. The completion of Christ's reign is seen in his victory over death, the ultimate enemy power (1 Cor 15:26). As many scholars have suggested, vv. 51–56 indicate that this is another way of describing the resurrection of the dead. V. 57 describes the event as the victory of the faithful, i.e., as God's giving them victory through Christ.

We have also seen that the ultimate purpose of the reign of Christ is to establish the kingdom of God, i.e., to bring all things and everybody to God, so that God may be all things to all (1 Cor 15:28). In that event the resurrection of Christ as well will reach its ultimate completion and purpose. The apostle locates the completion at the parousia, i.e., at the coming of Christ in the end-time. He insists on this. The coming of Christ will be the culmination of the lordship of the risen Christ.

The Resurrection of Christ, the Present Christian Existence, Death, and the Future Life

Our analysis of 1 Corinthians 15 has brought out that Paul does not emphasize the present saving reality, but that elsewhere, when he is freer, he does relate the resurrection of Christ to the present Christian existence and even emphasizes it. He sees the power of Christ's death and resurrection operating in the lives of the faithful; he talks about dying and rising with Christ.

Yet the resurrection of the faithful remains for the apostle an *end-time* reality not to be fused with the present life of faith. He never talks about the latter as if it were the risen life, and in 1 Corinthians 15:24 he points out the difference between Christ's resurrection and that of the faithful: "But each in his order: Christ the first fruits, then at his coming those who belong to Christ." The present life of faith is thus not yet the risen life. Here, as in 1 Corinthians 15:51–55, 2 Corinthians 4:14 and Philippians 3:20–21, the resurrection of the faithful is associated with the coming of Christ in the end-time and with transformation of the present existence. Paul has apparently corrected an attempt in Corinth to reinterpret the end-time resurrection in terms of the present experience of faith (1 Cor 15) or as a purely spiritual existence outside the body beyond one's death (2 Cor 5:1–10). This is generally admitted by scholars, although some of them in practice fuse the resurrection with the life of faith.

Nowhere does the apostle interpret the death of the faithful as the experience of the resurrection. In 1 Thess 4:13–18 he con-

soles the grieving faithful that their deceased friends, who believed in Christ, will share in the glorious coming of the Lord in
the end-time. In 1 Corinthians 15 and in 2 Corinthians 4:14, as we
have seen, he talks about the end-time resurrection of the dead.
Only in Philippians 1:21–23 does he expect to be with Christ immediately upon death. Did he here shift to the Hellenistic anthropology? J. Dupont and others hold this opinion even concerning
2 Corinthians 5:1–10, whereas Hoffmann has pointed out that
Paul has retained his Jewish anthropology in all his letters.[4] The
apostle expects throughout his correspondence the resurrection of
the dead and the coming of the Lord in the end-time. Philippians
1 suggests an interim existence as a heightened union and association with Christ, but its framework is still Jewish apocalyptic,
which allows for such existence. According to Beker,[5] Jewish
apocalyptic is the only appropriate framework for Paul's proclamation of the end-time realities. The apostle apparently found the
Hellenistic frame of thought inappropriate for conveying the full
meaning of the Christ event.

Paul thus has a picture of the world and of history that is ap-
proaching its end and its culmination. However, in presenting the
Christian completion he modified the traditional apocalyptic view
and strongly reduced its scenery to fit the one essential fact—
union and association with Christ. This concentration on Christ is
a profound change in the apocalyptic perspective, which has nothing comparable. For the apostle, salvation is in being with Christ.
His presentation of the Lord's coming, of the final resurrection,
and of life with Christ after death are unique features in the general
apocalyptic framework.

Some scholars regard Paul's notion of the culmination in the
end-time as part of his outmoded apocalyptic perspective. They
therefore try to reinterpret the parousia and the end-time resurrection by relocating them either in the present life of faith or in the
encounter with God at one's death. What they say about these

things, however, depends heavily on the model they use and on their underlying philosophical system.

Models of the Resurrection

We shall try here to indicate very briefly four ways in which Pauline presentation of the resurrection and of the end-time coming of the Lord have been reinterpreted. We can speak of the models of Barth, of Bultmann, of J. Moltmann and of G. Lohfink.

a. Barth's Model[6]

In the 1920's Barth subscribed to the dialectical theology which placed man and God at opposite poles. According to this view, mankind is wholly in the bondage of sin, death and nothingness. The God who confronts a human person is wholly other. He is the Creator who through his revelation and his sovereign salvific activity brings about in the human being a new creation. Barth constructed his model from the point of view of God's self-revelation.

It is this life from God's hands, as God's self-revelation given to the person, that Barth at this period of his thought called the resurrection of the dead. It is not a change in the person's physical existence but a spiritual life that through God's grace alone is presently taking place in the believer. The phrase "resurrection of the dead" thus expresses the absolute contrast between the former lifeless condition of the person and the present life in faith. It also emphasizes the absolute transcendence of God's saving activity. At this period Barth held the biblical notion of the resurrection to be a mere figure of speech.

Later on Barth modified this view somewhat. He acknowledged that, in the instance of Christ, the resurrection was complete in the biblical sense, but he continued to regard the resurrection of the faithful as before, i.e., as describing the present existence in faith.

Still later Barth held that the believer's resurrection is something incomplete, but only in the sense that it has not yet been revealed. The future revelation, however, will only disclose what is already present now.

According to G. Greshake,[7] Barth in his latest letters, apparently admitted that there is a more profound incompleteness in the present saving experience. The fulfillment is yet to come and is given to the believer in the present only as a promise.

Greshake[8] has pointed out that this strongly-unified and systematic perspective, depending as it does on Hegel's idealistic thought, barely tolerates the data of biblical revelation. History and humanity are not given their due place in this scheme. We miss here the cosmic dimension of God's victory, strongly emphasized recently by Beker, and Paul's affirmation and meaning of the end-time coming of the Lord.

b. Bultmann's Model[9]

Bultmann, as Greshake[10] has observed, also began with dialectical theology but, in contrast to Barth, whose perspective was God's self-revelation, he began with man's conscious existence in faith. He took up and modified Heidegger's existentialist philosophy which understands a person's conscious presence in the world as a responsible existence. An individual through responsible decisions appropriates his own possibilities and so transcends his inauthentic and closed existence and embraces the future. Here the person's former closed existence is but a stage in becoming, to be overcome by the individual's own efforts.

Bultmann brings to this system of thought the biblical data of the fall of man and of God's offer of salvation through Christ in the proclamation. In light of these data one cannot by one's own efforts abandon his former self and embrace the future, for the person is not free and must first be liberated. This occurs through

God's action in Christ which is effectively taking place in the proclamation. By a decision in faith the individual accepts this offer and relinquishes all anxieties and reliance on self and abandons himself to God and to the future offered by God. In this act of faith, which is at the same time an act of love, one's existence acquires its ultimate meaning.

This existence in faith is what Bultmann calls the risen life. His entire system of thought is focused on this event; the past and the future occur here. It is here that the resurrection of Christ and the ultimate completion take place. Yet this existence is open-ended, for it is not a firm possession of salvation forever but rather calls constantly to new openness toward God. This holds also for the moment of death. At that instant occurs one's last decision to live solely in dependence on God's grace, hence in ultimate openness toward God.

Bultmann denies relevance for today of the biblical understanding of the resurrection of Christ and of the end-time resurrection as well as Paul's affirmation of the end-time coming of the Lord. He therefore reinterprets them according to his existentialist mode. According to him, the future "resurrection" is only a continuation of one's total openness toward God. If it should occur in the biblical sense, it will not bring anything essentially new to the person. The end-time coming of Christ is an apocalyptic remnant to be discarded.

Greshake has noted that Bultmann's closed system of thought prevented him from giving the proper role to the biblical data of revelation. An essential part of Bultmann's analysis is his preceding reality criticism of the biblical data, his demythologization. His reasons for this, however, have not been universally accepted by scholars and have caused a long theological debate. In general his theory is more suitable to the fourth gospel than to Pauline theology. According to Beker, Bultmann reduced the resurrection of Christ "to an intrapsychic event or to an existentialist event, that is, to a new self-understanding in the world. It becomes the perception of the meaning of the cross and thus loses both its character as event and its temporal apocalyptic moorings.''[11] What is wrong with it is that it is severed from its temporal and cosmological framework, thus losing the correlation of Christ's resurrection with the age to come. ''Its cosmological aspect is not only individualized and spiritualized but its temporal aspect is also reduced to a 'postmortem' immortality of the soul.''[12]

c. Moltmann's Model

In contrast with the first two models, Moltmann[13] affirms the full biblical meaning of the resurrection and of the coming of the Lord. He especially emphasizes the latter. The Lord's coming is something new yet already promised in the resurrection of Christ. In that act all that has not yet reached its identity will be removed. This holds true also for God's relationship with the world, so that Moltmann can speak of the future of God, i.e., of God's coming into his own, and of the future of the world.

The starting point for Moltmann is the world—the becoming of the world. In this model, God, history and the future are taken together. God is the Lord of history and of the world. The future of the world lies within its own possibilities, whereas the future of God is in God's coming into the world and brings to the world what the world cannot achieve. Although the future of the world and the advent of God must be distinguished, ultimately the former is subsumed under the latter. The becoming of the world is directed toward the completion of time and the future of God, which is reached with the resurrection of the dead.

Moltmann draws out the implications of the coming of Christ for the life of the faithful. They should actively contribute to the integration of the world through faith, hope and love. This calls as well for a political engagement. They are to contradict the present alienation in the world through their creative contribution in the knowledge of the future resurrection of the dead.

Greshake has observed that each of these models has a different perspective and in each process and time have a different significance. For Barth they have their meaning in God's revelation, for Bultmann in man's existential decision in faith, and for Moltmann in the call to a creative engagement in the progress of the world. This leads us to the fourth model which differentiates between the mode of existence of God, man and man after death.

d. Lohfink's Model

According to Lohfink,[14] the preceding models account neither for the near awaiting nor for the future fulfillment. Bultmann has reduced the future to the open horizon in the present and Barth to the disclosure of the present reality. Both have emphasized the newness of the present existence in faith by applying to it the language of the resurrection. Lohfink approves of this, but finds it inadequate.

To incorporate the near awaiting as well as the future completion, which is not necessarily located in the end-time, Lohfink constructs a model that distinguishes between time, eternity and *aevum* and that accounts for the corresponding modes of existence, i.e., of the existence of man (in time), of God (in eternity), and of the resurrected ones (in *aevo*). Man, being in time, is not equally present to every event in earthly history. God, who transcends time, however, is equally present to every moment of our earthly history. From God's perspective, the completion of history does not take place at the end of history, but at every moment in its course.

The existence in *aevo* (a mode of existence which medieval theologians ascribed to angels) is the existence of the risen ones. It differs from the eternity of God in that it is created and sustained by the power of God. It differs from earthly existence by being outside time and space yet related to time and space. A person at the moment of death leaves behind all time and space and becomes instantly present to all events in time and space. After death that individual is not a pure spirit wholly dissociated from the world, but has brought along a piece of the history of the world. It is this that then relates that person to the whole of history, including its completion. This embraces also the universal judgment and the resurrection of the dead which Lohfink locates at the individual's death. From the earthly point of view, the ultimate completion is at the same time something that has happened and that is yet to happen. From the perspective of the resurrection (of the *aevum*), the two are not in opposition, but the event and the completion coalesce.

According to Lohfink, a direct encounter with God always presupposes the individual's death. The parousia of the Lord can therefore occur only to those who have gone through death. Yet it need not occur at the end of time, but at the death of the individual. Hence the resurrection of the dead, the entry into direct relationship with God, also occurs at that moment. The near awaiting can be sustained since the completion coincides with the moment of one's death.

Lohfink's construct is an improvement over the preceding models. He does not postulate the completion of history, as does Jewish apocalyptic, and leaves open whether life after death is truly a resurrection of the dead or the immortal existence of the soul. He has shifted the completion from the end-time to the moment of one's death and then from time to the *aevum*. The completion of history and salvation is thus strongly individualized. The cosmic dimension is represented only to the extent that it is present in the individual's existence. From the earthly perspective, at least, this solution does not allow for the completion of history and for God's victory over sin and death in the world. The world can continue indefinitely, marked by sin and by grace. Lohfink's construct makes it possible to think of the completion without the last intervention of God in the world, but cannot rule it out. The death of all is assumed here as in the Revelation of John, but not in Paul.

4
Justification by Faith

Present Situation

In the past, Paul's doctrine of justification by faith, more than any other theological issue, separated Protestant and Catholic scholars. These differed not only in what the apostle meant by this notion, but also concerning its role in Paul and in the entire New Testament. Each side drew upon its own tradition and brought to exegesis its own questions and concerns. Protestants approached it in the wake of Luther's discovery of this doctrine and of his particular understanding of it. Catholics have correspondingly remained within the framework set by the Council of Trent which challenged the reformers' position. Until recently the discussion had been carried out mostly in dialogue with opinions held within the same tradition.

On the Protestant side an enormous literature arose on this subject—an indication that, in this tradition, the topic remained relevant and central. As N.A. Dahl has observed, "for Luther and Lutheran confessions, this doctrine is not simply one doctrine among many; it determines the whole understanding of Christianity."[1] Here justification is the very basis of confessional difference.

This, however, does not mean that traditional positions had

not been questioned. Among Protestants especially, we find influential critics who shook the foundations of the traditional conceptions. Here we need mention only W. Wrede, A. Schweitzer, W.D. Davies, K. Stendahl, N.A. Dahl, and E.P. Sanders. Nor was Luther's exegesis of Paul maintained in all particulars. At the turn of the century there occurred a shift in understanding the phrase "righteousness of God." Whereas Luther held that it meant a person's righteousness *before* God (objective genitive), most scholars came to regard it as God's righteousness (subjective genitive) or righteousness from God (genitive of author or origin) or the like. Subsequently the apostle's view was made more precise through the study of the righteousness of God in the Old Testament, in Jewish apocalyptic and in the recently discovered Dead Sea Scrolls.

At present there are signs of more open positions taken by both Protestant and Catholic scholars. Some, and this even on the Protestant side, question Luther's understanding of Paul on this issue. Others dispute that the doctrine is central in Pauline theology, let alone in the rest of the New Testament. Still others have openly reexamined both positions against the texts and have reached in certain aspects a compromise solution. Here we can mention the contributions of K. Kertelge, J.A. Ziesler, Wilckens, J. Reumann and Fitzmyer.

A major impetus toward the present discussion came from E. Käsemann in 1961.[2] His proposal was adopted not only by members of his school, but also by others, both on the Protestant and on the Catholic side. Its echoes reverberate in most of the contemporary discussion on this topic.

The Two Positions

In order to better follow the trend in the present discussion, let us here briefly outline certain emphases characteristic of the Protestant and Catholic positions respectively.

On the Protestant side, justification by faith is usually singled out as *the* central theme in Paul and regarded as the apostle's gospel or close to it. It is a judicial act through which God, on the basis of Christ's saving death, grants to the sinner an undeserved gift of righteousness, or regards the sinner as righteous. This gift and pure grace is received through faith. It is opposed to works of the law. Many scholars extend this opposition to all works. The focus is on faith and grace. The anthropological side, i.e., man's cooperation with grace, is usually bypassed. The gift of righteousness calls for a new life in accordance with the grace received. Lately many scholars connect justification with life in Christ, the Holy Spirit, baptism and the Church.

Catholic exegetes, in contrast, usually regard justification by faith as *one* of Paul's themes. They do not single it out or regard it as central, rather they relate it to baptism, life in Christ, new creation, indwelling of the Holy Spirit, etc. It is one of the many metaphors describing the new Christian existence. They find the juridical interpretation and certain notions connected with it (imputation) inadequate and emphasize that the justified become really righteous, holy, transformed in the inner self and related in a new way to God. They grant that this is God's grace, but do not rule out man's cooperation with grace. They do not stress the opposition between justification and all works, as many Protestant scholars do.

Terminology

In English we have words like just, justice, justification, righteous, righteousness. There is no such distinction in the apostle's language. Some scholars (Ziesler) tend to use "righteous, righteousness" in an ethical sense, but this is not a common practice.

There is a biblical as well as a secular notion of righteousness. The two are not the same. According to the latter, one is declared righteous on the basis of fact: the person has been found innocent or in the right. But one is not "made righteous." Righteousness is not imparted or gained or reinstated or regained but rather recognized. Here a person is righteous when his or her behavior agrees with the established norm or the recognized ideal of justice. Thus for the Greeks both man and gods were righteous if their behavior agreed with the ideal norm of justice outside themselves.

However, in biblical language, God is said to be righteous in himself and in his acts. He reveals himself as righteous. But the measure of his righteousness is not outside himself. He acts righteously in accordance with his sovereign will. He is righteous toward Israel because he acts in agreement with the covenant he struck with Abraham, but that covenant is God's own sovereign decision and gift. Through it he makes it possible for Israel to be righteous with respect to himself.

In the Old Testament a person is said to be righteous when living in accordance with the covenant. One is thus declared righteous on the basis of fact.

In Paul, however, righteousness concerns man as a sinner. When God declares someone righteous it is not because he or she has been found in the right with God—that person is a sinner—but rather because of the saving death of Christ. By believing in Christ as God's offer of salvation, that person has been then set right with God. Some scholars say that one has been declared righteous, others that one has been made righteous.

Paul's Doctrine

The language of righteousness surfaces only occasionally in the apostle's letters outside Galatians and Romans. The peculiarly Pauline emphasis on faith and on grace occurs only in these two epistles. Hence these two letters become the focus of our attention.

In Galatia Paul had preached the gospel without forcing on the converts the law of Moses and circumcision. In his absence other Christian missionaries came in—most scholars hold that they were Jewish Christian Judaizers—and demanded that all comply with the law of Moses and accept circumcision.

The letter to the Galatians is the apostle's polemical response to this challenge to his gospel and to his apostolic authority. He understood that the opponents challenged the sole efficacy and sufficiency of the saving deed of Christ. In his eyes they have made the law, rather than Christ, the means of salvation. He therefore defends the authenticity of the gospel which he has preached, denies that there is any other gospel, and points out that faith rather than the law brought them the Spirit, made them sharers in the promise of Abraham, and adopted sons of God.

The main argument for justification occurs in Galatians 2:19–21, where Paul presents his own life in accordance with the gospel which he has preached. "For I through the law died to the law, that I might live to God. I have been crucified with Christ; it is no longer I who live, but Christ who lives in me; and the life I now live in the flesh I live by faith in the Son of God who loved me and gave himself to me. I do not nullify the grace of God; for if justification were through the law, then Christ died in vain."

We note that justification is here not singled out but rather mentioned together with the faith in the Son of God, the love of Christ, and the grace of God. It is opposed to the law. Life for God is thus a life by faith as opposed to the life by the law. Justification occurs apart from the law, by grace because of Christ's death.

In chapters 3–4 the apostle then brings out that faith rather than the law sets them right with God. They have received the Spirit by faith not by the law (3:2–4). With a scriptural argument he proves that Abraham was justified by faith in God's promise, not by the law. The promise made to Abraham has been fulfilled in Christ, and through Christ they themselves have become heirs to the promise. The law was given afterward because of transgressions. Its purpose was to restrain the people from straying, as one restrains an adolescent, and ceased with the coming into the world of God's Son through whom they have received mature sonship. Through the Son of God they have become "sons of God." "For in Christ Jesus you are sons of God through faith. For as many of you as were baptized into Christ have put on Christ. . . . And if you are Christ's, then you are Abraham's offspring, heirs to the promise" (3:27–29). They therefore need not fear that they are not true sons of Abraham. Through faith they have become Christ's and therefore Abraham's offspring and heirs to the promise. Through faith they have been also set right with God as "sons of God" and have received the Spirit: "And because we are sons, God sent the Spirit of his Son into our hearts, crying, Abba! Father! So through God you are no longer a slave but a son, and if a son then an heir" (4:6–7).

They have been thus set free of the law. Their conduct is to be henceforth guided not by the law but by the Spirit through which they kill the desires of the flesh (chapter 5).

The language of justification is not strongly present in Galatians. We do not find here the key expression "righteousness of God." However, all the elements of justification that we find in Romans occur here. A typical feature here is the emphasis on faith rather than on the law.

Some scholars question whether justification by faith is the central issue in this epistle (Schweitzer, Sanders). Others see Paul's peculiar emphasis here as merely a polemical response, hence only of historical value without a permanent theological significance (Wrede, Davies).

The apostle's main exposition of justification by faith occurs in Romans. It is here that he treats the theme in semi-isolation. The epistle is not polemical, as is Galatians. The main texts dealing with our topic are 1:17 and 3:21–26 (9:30–33; 10:1–13).

Having presented his gospel concerning Jesus Christ as the

Son of God, Paul states in 1:16–17 what most scholars regard as the theme of the entire epistle. ''For I am not ashamed of the gospel: it is the power of God for salvation to everyone who has faith, to the Jew first and also to the Greek. 17 For in it the righteousness of God is revealed through faith for faith; as it is written, 'he who through faith is righteous shall live.' '' Scholars are not unanimous whether the entire section is the theme (Käsemann, Wilckens), or whether the main theme is in v. 16 (Dahl) or in v. 17, i.e., whether the theme is the gospel or the manifestation of the righteousness of God.

We find here one of the key terms, ''righteousness of God.'' We observe that in this context it is related to the gospel which is the power of salvation and which is meant for Jews and Greeks. In the subsequent section, 1:18–3:20, the apostle then brings out the bleak background of sin among the Gentiles and the Jews, hence the world under God's condemnation.

In 3:21–26 we find what scholars regard as the central statement of Paul on justification by faith. The text takes up 1:17 and discloses God's action in Christ which redresses the sinful condition of the world. ''But now the righteousness of God has been manifested apart from the law, although the law and the prophets bear witness to it, 22 the righteousness of God through faith in Jesus Christ for all who believe. For there is no distinction; 23 since all have sinned and fall short of the glory of God, 24 they are justified by his grace as a gift, through the redemption which is in Christ Jesus, 25 whom God put forward as an expiation by his blood, to be received by faith. This was to show God's righteousness, because in his divine forbearance he had passed over former sins; 26 it was to prove at the present time that he himself is righteous and that he justifies him who has faith in Jesus.''

In view of the presence of sin everywhere God instituted his own righteousness in the world despite man and apart from the law. The emphasis here is on God and on the reception of the gift by faith. The righteousness that has been revealed is God's righteousness, for he is the source and the giver, he established it through the atoning deed of Jesus Christ, and he justifies the one who believes. Man can only receive it by faith as a free gift. Man's justification is thus God's work and a manifestation of God's righteousness. Many scholars (E. Lohse, Käsemann, P. Stuhlmacher, C. Müller, Kertelge, Reumann, Wilckens) see behind this passage a pre-Pauline tradition although they do not agree as to its extent and its meaning.

In chapter 4 the apostle repeats the argument in Galatians 3 that Abraham was declared righteous by God because he believed and not because of the law or of circumcision. In chapters 5–8 Paul passes on to the description of the present Christian existence, using other images and metaphors. The relationship between this section and chapters 1–4 is disputed. Many regard chapter 5 as transitional (Dahl, Sanders); others link it either to the preceding (Wilckens) or to the following section (Bornkamm, Marxsen, Schlier). Although the language of justification thins out in chapters 5–8, the theme is not entirely abandoned. Paul here points out that the new order of salvation abolished the old order based on the law. But he goes to the basic issue, to the power of sin. It is the hold of sin on man that has been broken. Because of this domination of sin, the law did not help man but played into the hands of sin. What had to be done was to break its hold on man, to heal man. This was done through the redemptive act in Jesus Christ. The believer is now under the power of Christ and of grace and freed from the power of sin (5:20; 7:5–25). In this new order the law is no longer needed, for the faithful are now guided by the Holy Spirit (8:1–17).

In chapters 9–11 the apostle deals with the problem of the refusal of the Jews to accept Jesus as the Christ. According to Paul, they strive for a righteousness of their own and have not submitted to the righteousness of God. Some scholars have seen this section as the center of the epistle (Stendahl), others have practically disregarded it, others again have integrated it under the theme of justification by faith.

In the last section, chapters 12–16, the theme of justification by faith is virtually absent except for a passing statement in 14:17. Those who make justification by faith the main theme in Romans interpret this section accordingly, i.e., as the righteousness of God in daily Christian life (Käsemann).

In Romans we find the same emphasis on faith as in Galatians, but a more profound insight into the power of sin, the universal sinfulness of man, the role of the law, and of the action of God in justification. God's part is brought out by the phrase "righteousness of God" as well as by the explicit affirmation of God's action in Christ's death, in the gospel, through grace and through the Holy Spirit. The law is not presented, as in Galatians, merely as a slave driver. It is exonerated as holy, good, and willed by God. Nevertheless, it was ineffective and usurped by sin. The difficulty is not in the law but in the flesh, the source of covetousness in man in the wake of Adam's fall, through which sin has a hold on the person. What the law could not do, God accomplished through the death of Christ. Christ died to sin and to the law. Through baptism, by belonging to the body of Christ, the faithful share in this death to sin and to the law. They now belong to the power of Christ and are given the Spirit by which they put to death the old self. In Christ and with the Spirit dwelling in them they are now God's children and heirs.

Recent Interpretations

We have seen that in the past the discussion revolved around the phrase "righteousness of God." The meaning righteousness before God has been abandoned and most scholars now hold that it means God's righteousness or righteousness coming from God. There is a growing consensus that it is not an attribute of God but rather a reference to God's activity. Related to this is the old confessional problem whether justification is a judicial act or whether it involves a real change in the person. In the wake of Schweitzer the discussion continues about its place in Pauline theology and its relationship to ethics.

Recent discussion is to a large extent carried on in the wake of Käsemann's suggestion (1961) that put an end to the debate about the genitive in the phrase "righteousness of God."[3] Käsemann has shown that the distinctions of grammar only cover the underlying views. He also moved away from the individualistic interpretation of justification by faith as held by the Bultmann school and stressed the corporate dimension, the body of Christ. Käsemann was followed closely by Müller and Stuhlmacher. Kertelge, a Catholic, found his proposal a promising new beginning. We find a strong influence of Käsemann also on Ziesler's ecumenical study, on the commentaries on Romans by Schlier and Wilckens, and on Reumann's ecumenical dialogue. As recent critical investigations that question the established view, especially that of German Lutheran scholars, and to some extent also Käsemann's interpretation, we may mention here the contributions of Stendahl, Dahl and Sanders.

Käsemann's Proposal

Käsemann took the expression "righteousness of God" as a stereotyped phrase which Paul found in tradition and in Judaism. Instead of a grammatical or an historical explanation he proposed a theological interpretation. He suggested that the uniquely Pauline element in the righteousness of God is power, as Romans 1:17 indicates. Here the gospel is said to be the power of God because in it the righteousness of God is revealed. Käsemann points out that power is associated with the Holy Spirit, with the lordship of the risen Christ, and with grace. Under a certain aspect these realities are identical. They express Paul's understanding of the God who ''is manifest in his creation in judgment and grace, and who acts in relation to it as Lord.''[4] Accordingly, ''righteousness of God . . . speaks of the God who brings back the fallen world into the sphere of his legitimate claim.''[5] The Lord is God's eschatological saving gift to us, and at the same time his rightful claim to us.

Justification as power has been accepted for Romans 1–3 by Schlier, Wilckens and Kertelge, although many scholars found it less appropriate as a general characteristic of the righteousness of God and have modified it accordingly. Käsemann's proposal is not entirely original, for it was made already by Cerfaux. However, it provided a way out of the debate whether righteousness of God is juridical or real (effective). The two need not be in opposition. Pauline vocabulary suggests a juridical structure but power indicates the effectiveness of God's righteousness. It is more than a mere imputation. Käsemann's students Müller (1964)[6] and Stuhlmacher (1966)[7] adopted it with some modifications. Stuhlmacher prefers to speak of the right and the faithfulness of the Creator toward his creation and of his saving action rather than judgment. For Käsemann and his school, justification by faith has a univocal meaning and is central not only in Paul but in the entire New Testament.

Whereas Käsemann's solution has many valid points, his emphasis on power and judgment can scarcely be maintained. Power is in fact more closely and directly associated with the proclamation of the gospel, with the Holy Spirit, and with the lordship of Christ than with justification proper. The death of Christ, to which justification is related, is for the apostle not merely judgment, but above all a manifestation of God's and Christ's love for us, as Romans 5:6–10, 8:31–32, and Galatians 2:20 indicate. Moreover, the Holy Spirit is not only a power but also the outpouring of God's love. In Paul the power of God is not opposed to the love of God.

An Ecumenical Study on the Catholic Side

Kertelge,[8] a Catholic, took up Käsemann's solution and incorporated it with certain modifications. His own position is open and sympathetic to the Protestant view and embraces critically much of the traditional Catholic emphasis as well. His book is quoted with approval by many Protestant scholars. In the wake of Käsemann, Kertelge focuses on the expression "righteousness of God" which he, too, regards as a stereotyped phrase. He finds the specifically Pauline notion of justification in Romans 1:17 and 3:21–26. However, for him, Käsemann's emphasis on power is too restrictive and he has proposed instead the notion of activity. Accordingly, the righteousness of God expresses God's saving activity with respect to man which is the basis of a new relationship between man and God. It may even mean that new reality (2 Cor 5:21). It is thus an attribute neither of God nor of man. It embraces two mutually related and inseparable components, the revelation of the Christ event in the death of Christ and in the proclamation as well as faith. Justification is basically the new relationship which becomes a reality only when the revelation has been accepted by faith. It means that the sinner has been declared and effectively rendered righteous. Kertelge stresses that this is an end-time (eschatological), creative and mighty activity of God, i.e., when it takes hold of man, it puts an end to the old aeon marked by law and sin and recreates the person by bringing about a new relationship with God.[9]

According to Kertelge, Paul brings here to the language of the Old Testament, of Judaism and even of the early Church a new meaning. In the Old Testament God's righteousness was his saving activity which makes possible or restores his covenant relationship with Israel. It is basically God's covenant faithfulness. In the Dead Sea Scrolls, where we find many affinities with the Pauline notion, as well as in the rest of Jewish apocalyptic, righteousness was totally determined by the law. In the early Church's view as seen in the pre-Pauline tradition in Romans 3:24–26a, it meant a restoration of the covenant on the basis of God's act in Christ through which past sins have been atoned for and forgiven. The apostle, however, stresses, beyond the forgiveness of sins, the re-creation.[10]

Kertelge agrees with most Protestant scholars that justification by faith is central to Pauline theology since it is an application of the gospel. It is not merely a time-conditioned and polemical response but has a permanent validity in that it calls for obedience in faith.[11] Against the traditional Catholic linking of justification with baptism he states that the apostle himself, in contrast with the pre-Pauline tradition, does not link justification directly to baptism. However, Paul does not know of any faith apart from baptism.[12] The usual Protestant explanation that a person is declared righteous is acceptable when we understand that declaration is effective. The power of God is effective. The one who has been declared righteous is no longer a sinner but is placed in a new relationship with God.[13] Kertelge defends the juridical meaning of righteousness on the basis of the Septuagintal usage of the vocabulary involved, but denies that it has an independent significance for the apostle. The function of the juridical imagery is to bring out God's sovereign and creative dispensing of salvation.[14]

Kertelge's solution is more balanced than Käsemann's. The widening of the aspect of power to activity, the omission of the emphasis on judgment and the emphasis on the effectiveness of declaration have a better exegetical foundation. His description of the pre-Pauline notion of justification as a restoration of the covenant, based on Romans 3:24–26a, however, is overdrawn. As the statement "This cup is the new covenant in my blood" found in the eucharistic tradition in 1 Corinthians 15:25 indicates, the pre-Pauline tradition was aware of the new covenant. His argument that justification is central to Pauline theology because it expresses the gospel does not effectively counter a similar claim made by Schweitzer concerning the mystical union with Christ. That the pre-Pauline tradition rather than that Paul connected justification with baptism is a tenuous argument, for the apostle quotes this tradition as agreeing with his own view. It is interesting to observe the reverse tendency among Protestant scholars to relate justification by means of the motifs dying and rising with Christ and incorporation into the body of Christ to baptism and to Church.

An Ecumenical Study on the Protestant Side

On the Protestant side Ziesler[15] undertook a similar ecumenical study. His explicit intention was to provide a solution that would incorporate as much as possible of both Protestant and Catholic positions and that would also bridge the divisions within the Protestant exegesis. In particular, Ziesler tried to meet the objection of Schweitzer that justification does not lead to ethics. If one is justified as the Protestant exegesis of that period held, i.e., having been declared judicially righteous but in fact remaining a sinner, then how can that person posit ethical acts? Schweitzer has pointed out that Paul does not derive ethics from justification but rather from union with Christ. This objection of Schweitzer has forced many Protestant scholars to see justification no longer in isolation, but together with other expressions describing Christian existence (dying and rising with Christ, being "in Christ," belonging to the body of Christ, baptism, etc.).

Ziesler's approach was to provide a linguistic evidence that justification means both a judicial declaration and an ethical renewal. According to him, statistical evidence shows that, in the Old Testament and Judaism, the verb "to justify" usually means to declare just or righteous rather than to make righteous, whereas the noun and the adjective imply ethical behavior. The latter two denote a way of acting that is appropriate to the covenant or that is within the covenant relationship. Only very seldom does the verb mean "to make righteous." In the Hebrew bible it indicates a restoration to a position within the covenant or within the covenant community.[16]

Assuming that Paul would use these expressions in the established sense, Ziesler then shows that the apostle's idea of justification supports partially both Protestant and Catholic views. The verb "to justify" accordingly means "to declare just or righteous," not "to make righteous" or "to impart righteousness." The noun and the adjective, in contrast, imply a right behavior. The latter fact thus roots ethical activity in justification, vindicates partially the Catholic position and removes the objection of Schweitzer. Ziesler also shows that the texts dealing with justification lead to incorporation into the body of Christ and to solidarity with Christ. The believer shares in the death and resurrection of Christ which Paul also understands in an ethical sense.

Thus Ziesler concludes, "If we take the verb as essentially relational and forensic, and the noun and adjective as describing behavior within the relationship and if we also make full use of the corporate Christ idea, we arrive at an exegesis which satisfies the concerns of both traditional Catholicism and traditional Protestantism."[17]

Ziesler's ecumenical openness, welcome as it is, meets at best only a minor part of what Catholic scholars affirmed using the expression "imparted" or "made righteous." For them, these words imply the whole new being in Christ, the new relationship, the new creation, in which ethical uprightness is made possible and is required. The differences between the Protestant and the Catholic position are often only in terminology. There remain two difficulties with Ziesler's solution. Although he himself states that the verb in Jewish apocalypticism lost its juridical meaning, he affirms the juridical meaning for it in the general summary and proceeds on the assumption that Paul used it in that sense. Secondly, the apostle's use of the verb in Romans 3:22–23, according to Ziesler, is "bold." It means, "restoring the relationship in which man may be righteous."[18] As Kertelge has shown, it probably means more than a mere restoration. At any rate, the meaning of the verb comes close to the sense "to make righteous." Since the meaning of righteousness in Paul here is different from that in Judaism, including the Septuagint, we may expect some difference in the use of the vocabulary.

Some Critical Contributions

Here we can mention the contributions of Stendahl,[19] Dahl[20] and Sanders.[21] They are all critical of the established Protestant exegesis.

Stendahl has reexamined the usual Protestant understanding of justification in the wake of Luther. According to him, Luther's question "How can I find a gracious God?" belongs to the introspective conscience of the west rather than to Paul who enjoyed a robust conscience. An historical analysis of Romans discloses that the apostle was not concerned with the above question, nor even with the universal sinfulness of man. Rather, he tried to provide a basis for the presence of both Jews and Christians in the Church. The one theme that is sustained throughout Romans is "Jews and Gentiles." The center of Romans is in chapters 9–11 which deals with this relationship and with God's plan of salvation. Paul's argument is that "since justification is by faith it is equally possible for both Jews and Gentiles to come to Christ."[22] He does not emphasize the juridical righteousness, as did early Judaism, but rather salvation, rescue, victory and triumph.[23]

Dahl finds Stendahl's solution too radical in some respects, although his own proposal is close to it in many ways. According to him, the central issue in Romans is not the apostle's defense of his Gentile mission but rather his missionary theology.[24] The main theme in the epistle occurs in 1:16: The gospel is God's power of salvation for Greeks as well as for Jews. This coincides with Paul's missionary gospel. The subthemes, occurring in the next verses, are that in the gospel the righteousness of God is being revealed as well as the wrath of God against all ungodliness.[25] In Dahl's view, the early Church regarded the historical event of Christ's death and resurrection as a turning point and a saving event. It was a change of aeons. The covenant here is not the renewed covenant, as in the Dead Sea Scrolls, but the new covenant in Christ's blood. Members participate in it by sharing in Christ's death and resurrection. Dahl admits that the specifically Pauline emphasis on faith to the exclusion of works is polemical. However, its application in Romans is not polemical but rather an essential component of his missionary theology. He agrees with Stendahl that it is not intended to answer troubled consciences. According to Dahl, it speaks to the fear of the Gentile Christians that they are second class members in the Church and that their lack of circumcision jeopardizes their relationship with God. Paul's concern is with unity in the local congregation and in the entire Church.[26] Dahl's observation on the early community's notion of the righteousness of God (a new covenant in Christ's blood) puts in question Kertelge's description of it as the restoration of the covenant. The analysis of the thematic and epistolary structure of Romans counterbalances Käsemann's extreme emphasis on justification by faith as the organizing principle of the epistle.

Sanders is even more critical of the established Protestant view, especially that held in Germany, than are Stendahl and Dahl. He also shows an ecumenical openness toward Jews. In much of this he follows his teacher Davies. His approach, however, is fresh: he compares the whole pattern of thought in Paul with that on the Palestinian Judaism of that time. He tries to answer three basic questions: How does one get in? How does one stay in? What is the goal of religion?[27]

According to Sanders, the meaning of righteousness by faith can only be explained from the two primary convictions of the apostle, the salvific role of Christ and his own call to be an apostle to the Gentiles. From the conviction that Christ died for all, the apostle drew two consequences: that Christ's death was necessary, and that all needed to be saved. The death of Christ therefore excludes all other ways of salvation, especially that salvation can come by way of obedience to the law.[28]

How in particular does righteousness by faith fit into this pattern of thought? According to Sanders, it is another way of expressing participation in the saving event, which is a more basic and all-embracing theme, as Schweitzer has shown. Righteousness by faith answers the question: How does one get in? It therefore deals with the transfer. However, it is only one of the transfer terms. Other such terms are: participation in the death of Christ; freedom from the bondage (of sin and of the law); transformation; new creation; reconciliation.[29]

In contrast to the early Church's understanding, Paul brings out the opposition of the righteousness by faith to the righteousness by the law. Justification cannot come in any other way except through Christ. The argument that it comes through faith is an argument against the law.

Galatians and Romans indicate that righteousness by faith is basically a negative and antithetical notion. The apostle does not work out its positive meaning. He employs both juridical and participationist language. Righteousness by faith is "*limited* to the forensic category of acquittal for past transgressions and sometimes explained by the participationist language which explains how one in Christ dies to the power of sin in order to live a new life to God."[30] When it is expressed in juridical language, it is not a transfer term. This, according to Sanders, shows that juristic language is not as fundamental as the participationist language.[31]

Paul's meaning of righteousness differs from that in Judaism. Here, according to Sanders, it expresses how one stays in (the covenant), whereas in Paul it answers the question how one gets in (Christ). This corresponds to the different goals of religion. For the apostle, the goal is Christ: to be found in Christ and attain, by suffering and dying with him, the resurrection.[32] Sanders, in the wake of Schweitzer, denies that righteousness by faith is the center of Pauline theology. The real center and one that agrees with the apostle's gospel is participation in Christ. Whereas Käsemann and his school as well as many others gave a unified meaning to righteousness by faith, Sanders finds that unity forced on the texts. He simply documents a variety of usages of this concept in Paul.

Together with Stendahl and Dahl, but for different reasons, Sanders again raised the question forcefully put by Schweitzer about the central role of justification in Pauline theology. It challenges Käsemann's, Stuhlmacher's and Kertelge's affirmation that it is central in Paul's thought. His definition of what he regards as central, i.e., the basic concept from which other theological aspects are derived, both forces a clarification in terminology and undercuts his own affirmation that participation in Christ is the center, for the latter is also derived from the death and resurrection and the lordship of Christ.

A welcome side of Sanders' exposition is his ecumenical openness toward Judaism. By presenting the pattern of religion in Palestinian Judaism he challenged the repeated affirmation of the Bultmann school and other German Protestant scholars who regard Jewish legalism as a self-affirmation and self-glorification before God. The absence of source criticism in the area of Jewish literature of that period, however, as Fitzmyer has pointed out, makes his description of the pattern of religion in Judaism rather tenuous.

Commentaries on Romans

Two major commentaries on Romans have recently appeared in German written respectively by Schlier,[33] a Catholic, and

Wilckens.[34] The latter commentary is part of the series Catholic-Protestant Ecumenical Commentaries. For Schlier, righteousness of God governs the epistle to the Romans. The theme of the epistle is the gospel as the power of God that brings about salvation to the believer and thereby makes manifest God's righteousness. Righteousness of God has a critical function and Schlier relates it, in agreement with Käsemann, with judgment. He takes the expression "righteousness of God" to be predominantly a subjective genitive. In Romans 3:21–26 the expression means more than mere forensic declaration, for it is effective in bringing about the change in the sinner. Schlier denies that 3:21–26 contains a pre-Pauline tradition. In many respects Schlier's view is close to Käsemann's.

Wilckens also agrees on many points with Käsemann but brings out the aspect of love often emphasized by Catholic scholars, particularly by S. Lyonnet, and disputed by Käsemann. Concerning human cooperation with the grace of justification—a touchy issue with most Protestant scholars—Wilckens is not as sweeping as many other Protestant scholars. Ziesler, for all his ecumenical efforts, still asserts: "It all rests entirely on his grace, our faith being not the ground but the means by which justification operates. . . . This entire dependence on grace is not only initially, at baptism or conversion, but remains. Even after a lifetime of Christian service, the believer has no works on which to rely. Justification is always by grace through faith, now, and before God's judgment throne."[35] Wilckens removes all cooperation on the part of man as held by the Pelagians or the nomists in the Middle Ages or as assumed by the penitential practice in the late Middle Ages, but does not criticize the official Catholic teaching on this point.

An Ecumenical Dialogue

Here we can mention the Lutheran-Catholic dialogue on justification. The Lutheran side is presented by Reumann, the Catholic by Fitzmyer and J. Quinn.[36] In the section of his presentation that deals with Paul, Reumann often takes issue with the more liberal views of Ziesler and Sanders. His own position agrees substantially with Käsemann's and Kertelge's. For him, justification by faith is not limited to the polemical section in Paul and did not arise as a response to the Judaizers. Against Sanders he maintains that justification is *the* central theme in Pauline theology, but without effectively challenging Sanders' position based on his definition of what he means by "central." Against Sanders he also maintains that justification is more than merely the initial transfer. However, Reumann admits that justification is not part of the message of Jesus; it appears rather in sections that bring out the significance of the death and the resurrection of Jesus.

Fitzmyer agrees with Reumann on many points but also raises a number of reservations. He questions the extent of the pre-Pauline material adduced by Reumann and points out that the terminology of justification in this area does not yet have the specifically Pauline emphasis on faith apart from the works. Whereas Reumann integrates the reality of justification with other aspects of Christian existence, Fitzmyer warns against confusing the metaphor of justification with other metaphors describing Christian existence. He agrees with Reumann against Sanders that participation in Christ is not the center of Pauline theology, but is skeptical about Reumann's affirmation that justification is the center.

As this critical review of the discussion concerning righteousness by faith indicates, the issue remains lively and important. A better idea of how Paul understood this notion would help us in our present ecumenical efforts. It has become apparent that he is at times still interpreted in the light of a particular confession. Here a critical assessment by scholars from other traditions helps to redress the balance.

We have seen that Käsemann's solution corrected the undue emphasis which Bultmann placed on the individual and opened the way to the understanding of the corporate dimension of justification. This direction was taken up not only by his own school but also by others and moved Protestant exegesis closer to the Catholic position. Concerning some other matters, e.g., the stress on judgment, Käsemann's opinion needs to be balanced. In this respect Wilckens' interpretation, especially coming from another Protestant, provides a welcome corrective. The focus on power that Käsemann advocated was accepted by many scholars as valid within certain limits. It opened the path to the effectiveness of the word that declares a sinner justified. Kertelge, a Catholic, used this notion to bridge the difference regarding justification as "imputed" or as "imparted." Within certain limits Catholic scholars have accepted the juridical character of justification.

The investigation of the apostle's "pattern of religion," which Sanders undertook, yields further insights into the place of justification in Paul's notion of salvation. Sanders' definition of what he means by "center" has clarified the terms of the discussion. When we apply this understanding to the discussion concerning the central place of justification in the apostle's theology it becomes clear that justification is not the center in this precise sense.

5
The Cross

Another important aspect of Pauline theology is the cross. The word "cross" is used metaphorically. It occurs on the lips of Jesus in the gospels and is found also in Paul's epistles. It refers to Jesus' death on the cross as willed by God and as God's way of salvation to be appropriated by Christians. All New Testament writers understand it in this fundamental sense.

Beyond this, John and Paul understand the cross as a cosmic and all-inclusive event within the dualistic structure of the cosmos. In this happening the powers hostile to God have been conquered and their dominion stripped away. It is at the same time the beginning of the dominion of the risen Christ meant for the entire human race.

The apostle underlines this meaning of the cross by employing also his own patterns of thought. He speaks of Christ as the second Adam, and of dying and rising with Christ. The cross means dying to sin, to the flesh, to the law. He appeals to the cross not only in preaching self-abnegation but also in calling on believers to change their human perspective for that of God.

The Inclusive Nature of Christ's Death

a. Christ as the New Adam

Paul regards not only the resurrection of Christ, but also the death of Christ as an inclusive event, i.e., as one embracing others and to be shared by all. 1 Corinthians 15:3, the eucharistic tradition in 11:24 and the traditional fragment in Romans 3:24–25 indicate that he shares this significance of the death of Christ with early Christian tradition. 1 Corinthians 15:3 and Romans 3:24–25 root this meaning of Christ's death in the will of God. That the apostle agrees with this is clear from 2 Corinthians 5:14, "We are convinced that one died for all; therefore all have died" (cf. Gal 4:4; Rom 8:3–4). Romans 5:8–11 and 8:31–32 present the death of Christ as not merely God's judgment, as some would have it, but as the supreme act of God's love for us.

Paul underscores this inclusive and universal significance of Christ by means of the parallel Adam-Christ. In 1 Corinthians 15:21–22 he compares Adam's transgression with Christ's resurrection, whereas in Romans 5:12–21 he compares Adam's sin and Christ's death: as through Adam came sin and death to all, so through Christ's death came grace and righteousness to all. According to R. Tannehill, this pattern of thought underlies also Romans 6:1–11.

b. The Two Dominions

Another means by which the apostle brings out the inclusive and universal meaning of the Christ event is the notion of two dominions. This resembles the dualistic structure of John's thought and is not peculiar to Paul, as Tannehill[1] would have it.

This pattern of thought brings out the change in the power structure in the world and in the cosmos. On the one hand there is the power of sin, death, the flesh and the law,[2] and on the other there is the power of God, of his Christ, of grace and of the Holy

Spirit. The two sets of powers act in unison, are opposed to each other and each has its exclusive domain. Each dominion influences the entire human race and the cosmos.

The Christ event brought about a change in the power structure that had prevailed since Adam. The old age, ruled by sin and its accomplices, has come to an end; the new age has arisen with Christ. The end-time reality, though not yet in its complete form, has begun.

The notion of two dominions, which is not the apostle's expression but which underlies his thinking, indicates the conflict of the two spheres of powers which "reign" or have dominion over the human race. God has through Christ, his Son, specifically through Christ's death and resurrection, conquered the powers that had subjugated the human race. He stripped them of their strength though he did not as yet annihilate them, and set up a new and end-time dominion governed by the risen Lord. The people who had been subjected to the unwholesome powers have been liberated from their overlordship. Those who believe in Christ have been transferred to his dominion and belong to him. They are in Christ, have the Holy Spirit in them and are destined for eternal salvation in the end-time.

In this pattern of thought, sin is not merely a transgression or a series of transgressions, but a power. People live in sin, i.e., belong to the domain of sin, and sin lives in them, exercising its baneful power within their very being. The same pattern holds true for Christ and the Holy Spirit. The faithful live in Christ and Christ lives in them; they walk by the Spirit and the Spirit dwells in them as a saving power.

As Tannehill[3] has observed, people are subject to either one or the other lord. Yet there is a difference which Tannehill has missed. The lordship of Christ and of the Spirit is not an oppression. Those who belong to Christ obey him freely, and those who have the Holy Spirit in them walk freely according to the Spirit.

Dying and Rising with Christ

To the inclusive reality of Christ's death and resurrection corresponds the dying and rising with Christ. What happened to Christ must happen also to those who believe in Christ. For Paul the universal offer of salvation through Christ becomes effective in the individual only through free incorporation into Christ and the conscious sharing of and assimilation into Christ's death and resurrection. As such it is also a sharing in the cross of Christ.

In Beker's view the cross is the apostle's apocalyptic interpretation of the death and resurrection of Christ.[4] It is, however, questionable whether the term "apocalyptic" is proper. It does not explain the inclusive nature of Christ. Moreover, the cross is not the fusion of the death and the resurrection. It is true that the language of the cross never occurs without an affirmation of life, but neither does the language of the death of Christ and of dying with Christ.

The basic text here is Romans 6:1–11. Paul reminds the Romans that baptism into Christ means a sharing in Christ's death (v. 3) in order to share also in his resurrection (v. 5). Although it is only in the future that the believer is to share fully in Christ's resurrection, he is to share in it also here and now, in Christ's life in the present. The apostle interprets this as the believer's conformity with the present life of the risen Christ to and for God.

Basic to this thought is Paul's understanding that God sent his Son—and not just *any* human being—into the world to share fully our human existence in the flesh and in the dominion of the powers of this world (Gal 4:4–5; Rom 8:3–7; Phil 2:6–11). In Romans 8:3–4 he states that God sent his Son "in the likeness of sinful flesh and for sin" to condemn sin in the flesh. Christ's death on the cross was thus a death to sin. In that act the power of sin lost its hold on him, and through him on all the rest of humanity. The believer, by being united with the crucified Christ, is liberated from the oppression of sin. The notion of two dominions and of the Adam-Christ parallel is here presupposed from Romans 5:12–21.

The point which the apostle wants to make here is that the believer is to die to sin in order to live to God, as the risen Christ lives to God, and Paul does this in vv. 10–11 by stating the purpose of Christ's death and resurrection. Christians are consequently not only drawn into the Christ event through baptism but are called to conform their lives to Christ's.

Yet how, precisely, does the believer die with Christ? This question plagued scholars for some time. Various solutions were proposed, such as: (a) Paul draws here on pagan mysteries; (b) dying with Christ is like a sacramental union; (c) dying with Christ is a "passion mysticism"; (d) dying with Christ and the death of Christ are contemporaneous or related to each other outside the time framework; (e) dying with Christ occurs through the pneumatic presence of the risen Christ in the faithful. R. Schnackenburg eventually suggested the notion of corporate personality, i.e., the Christ event represents and embodies many.[5] R. Tannehill agrees with this view and supports it with the idea of two dominions present in Romans 5 and carried over to Romans 6.[6]

Accordingly, the death of Christ broke the hold of the old dominion on the human race. Through baptism, or, more fundamentally, through faith, the individual is incorporated into Christ's death and resurrection, which means a transfer from the dominion of sin to the dominion of the risen Lord. The believer is henceforth determined by this founding and end-time event despite the temporal distance. Hence dying with Christ is not a repetition of the past event but a sharing in it.

How essential is this thought pattern? Where did the apostle obtain it? According to R. Bultmann, this pattern is not essential and can be reinterpreted. The dying with Christ occurs in the individual's response to the kerygma, when one accepts the crucified as Lord and lets go of his former way of thinking.[7] Tannehill and Beker, in contrast, emphasize that the thought pattern of two dominions brings out the objective and universal significance of the Christ event which are essential to Paul's thought. Beker[8] roots the thought in Jewish apocalyptic, whereas Tannehill suggests gnostic currents of thought. However, apocalyptic does not explain Paul's conviction that in Christ all have died and all have come to life. The roots of this thought seem to lie in the knowledge that Christ as the Son of God was sent into the world and for the world. We find this knowledge in the early Christian tradition, in John and, implied, in the synoptics. It has to do with the identity of Jesus and with his saving role.

Dying to the Law

This is the apostle's unique extension of the notion of dying and rising with Christ, applied originally to sin and to the flesh. As such it is part of his understanding of the cross. It is rooted in the knowledge that the Christ event brought about fundamental change in the situation of the world. The old oppressive structure, of which the law was a part, was destroyed and a new life, described as sonship (Gal 4:4–7; Rom 8:3–17), arose.

The question to ask here is: Why did Paul, in contrast to many others, conclude that the law has been abolished by the death of Christ? Was it because of the resurrection of Jesus? According to A. Schweitzer, the apostle's vision of the risen Christ had nothing to do with this, for others had had the same vision but had not come to that conclusion. Beker questions the correctness of Schweitzer's observation, pointing out that the Hellenists grouped around Stephen had already relaxed the law and embarked on the proclamation to the Gentiles.[9]

According to Beker,[10] Saul, prior to his meeting the risen Christ, saw a contradiction between the law, which curses everyone who hangs on a tree (Gal 3:13), and the crucified Messiah. The law apparently declared not only that Jesus was not a Messiah, but also that he was condemned by God. When Paul came

to know the risen Lord in his end-time mode of existence he realized that Jesus was confirmed and affirmed by God himself. He
concluded that the law came to an end in the crucifixion of Jesus;
for through the resurrection God not only confirmed the claim of
Jesus as the Messiah, but he also accepted the mode of his death.
The two are not contradictory.

This, as Beker recognizes, does not as yet mean that the law
came to an end for all. The resurrection of Jesus could still be regarded as invalidating the law for Jesus only: the law was wrong
in cursing the innocent one for being crucified. The crucifixion of
Jesus could be a miscarriage of human justice. The early Church,
at any rate, maintained just that. Another element was necessary
to make the abolition of the law valid for all. This element was
supplied, according to Beker, by the Antiochean Church which
held that Jesus died for all of us (Gal 3:13; 1 Cor 15:3). The apostle radicalized this confession to mean not only the forgiveness of
sins committed under the law, but the abolition of the continuing
validity of the law itself. The reason is that Jesus' death and resurrection initiate a new, end-time life in which mankind and God
meet under new conditions.

This reconstruction of Beker's needs to be supplemented by
Paul's statements in Galatians 4:4 and Romans 8:3–4. In both instances the apostle talks not of the Messiah but of the Son of God
whom he came to know at Damascus (Gal 1:16). This Son was
sent by God to share in our human nature and to live under the
law. According to Romans, God sent his Son for sin, to condemn
sin in the flesh, so that the just requirements of the law might be
fulfilled in us who walk by the Spirit. It was thus not the law that
was condemned in the death of the Son, but rather sin. However,
through the condemnation of sin in the flesh the law became su-
perfluous. The believers who are in Christ walk by the Spirit
which is opposed to the desires of the flesh and attunes the mind
to God.

This radical position with respect to the law brought Paul the charge that Christ is the servant of sin and that he, the apostle, condones sin (Gal 2:17; Rom 6:1). He consistently responds that the dying and rising with Christ means death to sin and to the flesh, and life with Christ to God (Rom 6:1–11). The believers are endowed with the Holy Spirit in whose power they desire and do what is spiritual and opposed to the desires of the flesh (Gal 5:16–26).

The abolition of the law does away with the election privileges of Israel. His position is that all have sinned and all need to be redeemed, both Jews and Greeks. The epistle to the Romans takes this as its starting point. Paul may have been interested in the abolition of the law for missionary reasons, although this was not his primary motivation. The mission itself springs from his absolute conviction that Christ died by the will of God to bring salvation to all and that he, Paul, was his apostle to the Gentiles.[11]

There is a continuing nervousness among scholars about Paul's bold position concerning the law. Many hold that the law as the holy will of God is still valid. According to Bultmann, only the cultic and ritual precepts of the law were abolished, while the moral precepts of the law remain valid.[12] The apostle, however, would not have understood these distinctions. In Romans 7:13, 14, 22 he affirms that the law is holy and the will of God, yet states that the believer is no longer governed by the law. The reason is that the faithful do the holy will of God not as an external commandment but spontaneously, through the inner dynamism of love and urged on by the power of the Spirit who dwells in them. According to 1 Thessalonians 4:6 the faithful need no instruction concerning brotherly love, for they have been taught by God in this regard (*theodidaktoi este*). Christians live for God following their new heart and the Spirit. S. Lyonnet gives a good example of this: As the mother who loves her child does spontaneously what is right for the child and needs no commandment "Thou shalt not kill," so also the believer who is attuned to God through the Holy Spirit needs no commandment to love, but does it spontaneously.[13] According to Paul, the person who loves fulfills the entire law (Rom 13:10).

The Challenge of the Cross

Paul's preaching of the cross as God's way in Christ and for the faithful is also a challenge to human perspective and worldly values. It counters this way of thinking in the faithful with the transcendent wisdom and power of God.

According to Beker, what the law is to the Jews, wisdom is to the Greeks. Both belong to the structure of the old aeon and must be destroyed. Against both prevails the apocalyptic element of negation in the cross.[14] There is some truth in this, although the division is not that clear-cut. In the Gospels this challenge of the cross is delivered in a Jewish context. Besides, the cross does not destroy the law itself but only human thinking determined by the law.

The apostle appeals to the cross to bring believers to humility and self-abnegation. The key texts here are 1 Corinthians 1:18–3:4, Philippians 2:1–11, and 3:17–19.

The context of 1 Corinthians 1:18–3:4 is provided by the sections that flank it, 1:10–17 and 3:1–4 (–4:21). Here we find that the Corinthians boasted of and took credit for their spiritual gifts. They formed rival factions, each glorying in its own leading figure, be it Christ, Cephas, Apollos, or Paul (1:10–17). Some attached too much attention to the proclaimers (3:5–9), others were fascinated by a "higher" wisdom that went beyond the fundamentals of the instruction in faith which they had received from the apostle (3:10–23). They thought they were already filled with perfection and power (4:8).

The community was richly endowed with spiritual gifts, yet was in a way still unspiritual. It measured spiritual matters by worldly standards, above all by wisdom and power. It is to change their entire perspective that Paul preaches the cross to them. In

1:18–19 he declares, "The word of the cross is folly to those who are perishing, but to us who are being saved it is the power of God. For it is written, 'I will destroy the wisdom of the wise and the cleverness of the clever I will thwart.' " The gospel of the cross is the cutting edge that separates those who are perishing from those who are being saved. Only to those who have experienced its saving power and who believe is the cross the transcendent wisdom and power of God. Others who have stumbled before it, as did some Jews, or have rejected it as intellectually unacceptable, as did some Greeks, find in the cross God's condemnation of their thinking.

Although the Corinthians have believed and have accepted the message of the cross, they have not yet fully appropriated it in their thinking and behavior. They have become proud even of their spiritual wisdom and power. The apostle therefore reminds them of their former nothingness and of how God, by calling them, shamed the noble, the wise and the powerful of the world. They have therefore no reason for boasting. Moreover, their present life in Christ is wholly a gift of God. Christ is to be by the will of God their wisdom, righteousness, sanctification and redemption. They are therefore to appropriate Christ to conform their thinking and their lives to Christ's.

Since they also misjudged his weakness and humility, Paul explains that he deliberately patterned his preaching to them according to the cross. He refrained from using "lofty words of wisdom" lest they should believe because of his powers of persuasion rather than because of the power of the Spirit working in him. Here and elsewhere he observes that the Spirit works best in human weakness. The proclaimer must not detract from the power and the glory of the gospel.

In Philippians 2:1–11 the apostle, striving to bolster unity in the community, presents to the faithful the cross of Christ from which they are to learn humility and selflessness. Christ did not cling to his divine prerogatives of honor and glory but emptied himself by assuming our human form, and went beyond that by becoming a servant and by being obedient unto death, "death on the cross" (2:6–8). The faithful should become Christ-like: they should let go of all selfishness, strive to be humble, and have the interests of others at heart. They should put on the mind of Christ (2:3–5).

The cross confronts not only human pride, but also human dissipation. In Philippians 3:17–19 Paul recalls with tears, "Many . . . live as enemies of the cross of Christ. Their end is destruction, their God is their belly, and they glory in their shame, with minds set on earthly things." He appeals to the faithful to imitate him (v. 17) by setting their minds on the world above and on the completion of their present existence through the resurrection-transformation at the coming of the Lord (vv. 20–21).

In all these texts the apostle presents the crucified Christ as the God-given way of salvation to be appropriated by the faithful. He himself is conformed to the cross of Christ, and calls on the believers to imitate him in this respect.

The Suffering Apostle

According to Beker, "the terminology of the cross is never directly related to suffering or to God's suffering."[15] We would agree with the latter but not with the former. Human suffering is part of the *theme* of the cross both in the gospels and in Paul even when the word "cross" is not used (1 Cor 2:3–4; 4:9–13; Gal 6:14–17). The apostle speaks of his own sufferings in the context of the cross.

It is mainly in 2 Corinthians that he talks of his sufferings as a sharing in the death of Christ. In a series of contrasting statements in 4:8–9 he links his afflictions and God's comforting. "We are afflicted in every way, but not crushed; perplexed, but not driven to despair; persecuted, but not forsaken; struck down, but not destroyed" (cf. 6:4–10; 11:23–33). He interprets these experiences as his "carrying in the body the death of Jesus, so that the life of Jesus might also be manifested in our bodies" (v. 10). His inner self is being thereby continuously renewed (v. 16). This suffering is part of his dying and rising with Christ. It not only intensifies his inner life, but it also brings life to the community, for it is endured in the service of the gospel through which grace is extended to many (v. 5; cf. 6:4–10). Because of God's comforting in the experience of the cross, Paul's hope in God has been deepened. In all this he is supported by the knowledge of the resurrection of the body. In v. 14 he declares, "He who raised the Lord Jesus will raise us also with Jesus and bring us with you into his presence." For this reason he affirms his conviction that the resurrection will involve the body (5:1–10).

The most poignant example of the apostle's suffering is given in 2 Corinthians 1:3–11. Here he reveals to the Corinthians that, when he was in Asia, he was utterly crushed, to the point of death (v. 9). Yet it was in that moment of being in the grip of death that he received God's help which he could never forget. He was raised to life again. It was like being raised from the dead. This profound experience gave him a new knowledge of the God who raises the dead to life and deepened his trust in God. "He delivered us from so deadly a peril, and he will deliver us; on him we have set our hope that he will deliver us again" (v. 10).

In the wake of this, Paul relied more than ever on God. He lived not from his own resources, but from the hands of God. His love of God reached a new intensity. In vv. 2–3 he talks tenderly about God as "the Father of mercies and God of all comfort, who comforts us in all our afflictions." Moreover, he drew a meaning from all this for his apostolic work and for his community. Having learned God's comfort, he now knows how to comfort others who suffer as he did. The apostle had to be taught how to comfort others. He also drew out of this the benefit for the community. "If we are afflicted, it is for your comfort; and if we are comforted, it is for your comfort" (v. 6).

The apostle invites the community to "patiently endure the same sufferings" (v. 6), for his hope is unshaken that they will also share in his comfort (v. 7). The experience of the cross unites him more closely not only to God, but also to the community.

Conclusion

It is clear that the cross is part and parcel of Paul's gospel. It is, however, not *the* gospel, as some scholars, especially of Protestant tradition, maintain, 1 Corinthians 1:18–19 and 2:2 notwithstanding. It is not the ultimate reality. Elsewhere the apostle preaches as his gospel the Son of God (Gal 1:16: Rom 1:3–4), the glory of Christ (2 Cor 4:4), and the death and the resurrection of Christ (1 Cor 15:3b–5).

Certain authors single out in this connection the *sola gratia*[16] and judgment. According to these, the cross is a condemnation of the way of the world and a call to live by grace alone, i.e., from the hands of God. This is true. However, the language of judgment is more appropriate to John's gospel than to Paul. Moreover, judgment is only one aspect of the cross. Another is the Father's and the Son's love for us (Rom 8:31–32). Furthermore, the cross cannot be correctly understood apart from the resurrection of Christ, the believer's rising with Christ, and hope in the resurrection of the body.

Paul sees in the crucified Christ God's negation of the way of the world. The cross is God's way of salvation and has a cosmic and universal significance. It is a liberating event in itself and not just in the believer's acceptance of the gospel. It changes not only the faithful's attitude toward God, but the state of affairs in the world. It strips the powers of evil of their hold on the human race.

The cross determines the message of the gospel, the messenger and the believer. The apostle's gospel is the gospel of the cross. It would not be the gospel without it. His life was a sharing in the cross for the sake of the gospel. He experienced in his own person the world's opposition to the message he proclaimed. Moreover, his gospel called for his conformity to the message he proclaimed. Similarly, the believer's life must be conformed to the gospel of the cross. Paul calls on the faithful to abandon the ways of the world and to become attuned to God. In particular, his is a summons to humility and selflessness in imitation of Christ and of himself. They are not only to imitate Christ, but to share in his cross. Only on the basis of the cross can the community achieve its unity in Christ.

Yet the cross is not merely an experience of dying. It redounds to life. This experience of life from God is a basis of hope and an affirmation by God. The community sustains the cross in the knowledge of the resurrection of the body. It knows that the last word of God is not the cross but life. It is to this hope of the faithful that we now turn.

6
Hope

The expectation of the attainment of the future realities of salvation comes up in a variety of contexts in Paul. We find the theme of hope present even when the word "hope" is not used. A comparison with other New Testament writings reveals that it is his major concern. One of his earliest interpreters, Luke, in the second half of Acts, often places this thought on the lips of the apostle. The structure of the present Christian existence as "already" and "not yet" contains a dynamic orientation toward the future. Both vectors are necessary for an authentic Christian hope. What is already given and experienced warrants confidence; what is still only promised draws beyond the present to the future completion.

We here present hope as a comprehensive framework of Pauline theology. It is an understudied aspect of Paul's thought and many questions still need to be asked. What is the basis of hope? To whom is hope given? To what is hope oriented? What is the role of Christ and of God in hope?

The Object of Hope

The apostle's hope, as Beker has brought out,[1] is directed to a variety of objects associated with his expectation of salvation.

They are all interconnected, and his focus usually depends on the context. The ultimate reality as the object of hope is the kingdom of God or the rule of God (1 Cor 6:10; 15:50; Gal 5:21). This is the underlying idea even when Paul does not use this stereotyped expression. In fact he uses it sparingly. In 1 Cor 15:28, e.g., he states that the culmination and the purpose of the risen Christ's lordship is "that God may be everything to everyone." It will be the experience of the utter fullness of God by all, and the victory of God through Christ over the hostile forces in the cosmos. As vv. 50–56 indicate, this includes the resurrection of the dead and the transformation. The apostle speaks also of the ultimate sharing of the glory of God (Rom 5:2), of the bestowal of the promised inheritance on the sons, of their final adoption (8:19, 23), of vision and understanding (1 Cor 13:10–12; 2 Cor 4:18), and of salvation (Rom 5:10). In 1 Corinthians 13:10–12, e.g., he states, "Now we see in a mirror dimly, but then face to face. Now I know in part; then I shall understand fully, even as I have been understood." Here and in 2 Corinthians 4:18 hope looks to the future, the eternal, the unseen, the incomprehensible. There is a yearning for the immediacy of union.

Since the entry into the kingdom of God is expected to take place through the coming of Christ in the end-time, the resurrection of the dead, and the union with the risen Lord, these future realities also belong to the goal of Christian hope and longing. We find the coming of Christ depicted in 1 Thessalonians 4:13–18. I have suggested that Paul here describes the parousia of Christ as a being taken up.[2] It was this particular presentation that caused the Thessalonians to worry about the possibility of the deceased faithful not sharing with the living in this glorious event—for one had to be alive to be assumed into heaven. The apostle assures them that, to the power of God, this is no obstacle: the dead will be brought back to life and then taken up together with those still living to be with the Lord for ever.

Usually, the end-time coming of Christ is associated with the resurrection of the dead (1 Cor 15:23–28) and the transformation of the present existence (Rom 8:23; 1 Cor 15:50–56; Phil 3:20–21). Whereas in 1 Corinthians 15 Paul affirms the transformation to brush aside any reservations about the resurrection, in Philippians 3:17–21 he points to the transformation as the known and expected future reality in order to direct the faithful from their fixation on this world to the world above. According to this text, the Lord himself will appear in the fullness of his power to transform our lowly bodies into the form of his body (vv. 20–21).

The apostle's personal hope and yearning for the resurrection and for conformity with Christ, which he shares with the faithful, occurs in 2 Corinthians 4:14–5:10. He groans for the completion, the glorious heavenly body of God's making. Even more than this, he desires to be at home with the Lord. His greatest pain is in his present partial separation from the Lord.

In contrast to this, Paul's hope is in Philippians 1:21–23 centered on being with Christ immediately upon death. As in 2 Corinthians 5, the present body means to him a separation from the Lord. He yearns to be with the Lord, for that is where his heart is: He welcomes death, for "to die is gain" and "to depart" means being with Christ.

The coming of Christ in the end-time, the resurrection and the transformation all have a salvific and redemptive significance for the apostle and as such are themselves fervently desired by him. Resurrection and transformation are not neutral happenings.

Paul's hope is thus characterized by his intense personal expectation of being with, sharing and beholding. This applies to Christ and beyond Christ to God the Father. It is this, above all, that explains his fervent expectation of the completion and his awaiting the near parousia. For the thoughts of the heart differ from those of the mind. The heart tends to bridge the distance and to foreshorten the time of separation.

The Subject of Hope

The goal of hope in effect also determines the subject of hope—those who believe in God, more precisely, those who believe in God's salvific action through Christ. This faith involves God the Father as the one "from whom are all things and for whom we exist," and Jesus Christ as the Lord "through whom are all things and through whom we exist" (1 Cor 8:6). Christ is for Paul God's agent in creation and above all in salvation (1 Cor 15:23–28). An essential part of Christian faith is the acknowledgement of Christ as God's Son. Only this disclosure of Christ's unique personal relationship with the Father fully convinces the believer of God's undying love, for he gave up his Son, whom he loves above all things, that we may have life (Rom 5:6–10).

An indispensable presupposition of the ultimate fulfillment is thus faith in and belonging to Christ. Hence the proper subject of hope is a committed Christian believer (1 Thess 4:13; 5:4–11).

The apostle therefore links hope with love and calls on Christians to live in love. "Love bears all things, believes all things, hopes all things, endures all things" (1 Cor 13:7). In 1 Thessalonians 1:3 he thanks God for "the work of faith and the labor of love and the steadfastness of hope" in the community. In the same letter he strengthens this hope (4:13–18; 5:9) and exhorts the faithful to "put on the breastplate of faith and love" (5:8).

Hope is informed by the knowledge, given to the faithful, of the mystery of salvation wrought by God in Jesus Christ. In 1 Corinthians 2:8–10 Paul declares that he imparts to believers "a secret and hidden wisdom of God for our glorification."

The promise of glorification is thus given only to those believers who live out their faith in love and so fulfill the one commandment of Christ and the will of God. The gift of the Spirit not only pours God's love into them, but it also guides and moves them toward love. The apostle therefore urges them to "walk by the Spirit" and not to "gratify the desires of the flesh" (Gal 5:16).

He warns repeatedly "that those who do such things shall not inherit the kingdom of God" (5:21). The faithful, those who in fact belong to Christ, "have crucified the flesh with its passion and desires" (5:24). They are not to fix their hearts on this world and its pleasures, but to accept the cross and focus on the heavenly realities yet to come, on salvation through the parousia of Christ when their lowly bodies will be transformed by his power (Phil 3:17–21).

It is in the experience of the cross that Paul himself has repeatedly felt the saving hand of God (2 Cor 4:7–12) and come to know the "God who raises the dead" (2 Cor 1:9), the Father of comfort and mercy (1:3–6).

The apostle on occasion threatens Christians with judgment and condemnation, as in 2 Corinthians 5:10, Romans 8:5–7, and 1 Corinthians 3:16, but he does this only to bring them back to their senses (1 Thess 5:1–10). Threats and fear (2 Cor 5:11; 7:1; Phil 2:12) are only peripheral to his thought. Paul usually exhorts and comforts the faithful. He prays for them that they may appear blameless at the coming of the Lord (Rom 15:13; 1 Thess 3:13). His central message is and remains hope, even as he calls for obedience to the Lord.

Although the apostle sees no hope for non-believers (1 Thess 4:13) and threatens sinful Christians with judgment and condemnation, he does not limit hope to believers only. In Romans 8:19–23 he draws the whole of creation into the expectation of hope, set up before the faithful. The entire cosmos is intensely interested in the prospect before the sons of God, for it hopes thereby to share in their glory and so escape from its own bondage to decay.

The Basis of Hope

On what, precisely, does Paul set his hope? We can answer this first negatively: not on himself or on any human effort. Positively, we can say that his hope rests in God and his Christ.

a. *God's Faithfulness, Love and Power*

According to the Old Testament, God has revealed himself to Israel as the one who chose his people, affirmed his faithfulness to them in the covenant, protected them, rescued them, and stood by them even when they disobeyed him. We may therefore agree with Bultmann that God was the hope of Israel.[3] However, this hope rests on Israel's concrete experience of God's faithfulness, love and power.

The apostle's hope is no different. The God in whom he believes is the "God of hope" (Rom 15:5), of truthfulness (1 Cor 1:9), of love (2 Cor 13:11), of mercy (Rom 15:9) and of power (Rom 11:23). It is the God who identifies himself with Christ. According to 2 Corinthians 1:10, all the promises of God have been fulfilled in Christ. We shall consider the love of God for us in connection with the death and resurrection of Christ. The power of God is at present working for our salvation through the risen Lord.

God's love, power and faithfulness are communicated also through the Holy Spirit. In Romans 5:5 Paul affirms, "And hope [of sharing the glory of God] does not disappoint us, because God's love has been poured into our hearts through the Holy Spirit." The gift of the Spirit is the guarantee that the faithful will in fact reach their destiny in God (2 Cor 5:5). The Spirit guides them in the way of salvation (Gal 5:16–24). In the power of the Holy Spirit they abound in hope (Rom 15:13).

The apostle often points out the faithfulness of God. He reassures the Corinthians, saying, "God is faithful, by whom you were called into the fellowship of his Son" (1 Cor 1:9). According to 1 Corinthians 10:13, God will not let the believers be tempted beyond their strength but will provide them with an escape.

b. *The Death and the Resurrection of Christ*

God's faithfulness, love and power are manifested in supreme fashion in the Christ event. Paul never tires of pointing this out. Since he telescopes this event into the death and resurrection of Christ, these and the ensuing lordship of Christ become the basis of hope.

The love of God for us through Christ and the love of Christ for us go together. This is shown most explicitly in Romans 5:6–10. The power of the argument here rests on the knowledge that Christ is God's beloved Son. It is only in God's handing over *this* Son for our sake that his love for us becomes fathomless and convincing. The fact that Christ died for the ungodly only strengthens the argument of God's love. He gave up his Son for us while we were as yet unlovable. This is the basis for the assurance that God will give salvation to the justified especially since this will be accomplished through his Son's life (v. 10).

This argument is summarized in Romans 8:32: "If God is for us, who is against us? He who did not spare his own Son but gave him up for us all, will he not also give us all things with him?" No charge against God's elect can hold, for it is God himself who justifies them. No one will condemn them, for Christ himself, who died, was raised, and is at God's right hand now intercedes for them (8:33–34). The believer is thus absolutely secure in the knowledge of God's and Christ's love.

There remains the threat that some distress or power or event in creation may separate the faithful from this love. The apostle assures them that they are "more than conquerors through him who loves us" (v. 37). Their strength comes from the Lord. They are not struggling alone. No power or happening in creation will be allowed to separate them from the love of God in Christ Jesus (vv. 38–39).

c. The Initial Fulfillment in the Present

According to Paul, the action of God in Christ extends into the present and implements the Easter event. God has placed the faithful in Christ (2 Cor 1:21), he has justified them on the basis of Christ's death (Rom 3:21–26), he has re-created them (2 Cor

5:17) and given them his Holy Spirit (Rom 5:5; 2 Cor 5:5; Rom 8:9–11, 26–27). All these realities have an end-time, eschatological significance. They represent the intrusion of the completion into the present. The justified have peace with God, have access to God, and rejoice in the expectation of salvation (Rom 5:1–2). Those who are "in Christ" are destined to be "with Christ" at his coming (1 Thess 4:13–5:11). The risen Lord himself is at present effectively carrying out his salvific role by the power of God (1 Cor 15:24–28). The presence of the Spirit in the believers is the guarantee that God will raise them from the dead through the same Spirit (Rom 8:10–11). The faithful are thus placed by God in the domain of salvation. They are those who are being saved (1 Cor 1:18). They are "sons of the day" (1 Thess 5:4–6).

The apostle, moreover, draws hope also from his own experience of God's help in his trials. Having received God's comfort in a situation in which he faced death he can then rely on further help from God (2 Cor 1:10).

All this represents a fulfillment of the promise of salvation in Christ's death and resurrection. As such it is a proximate ground of hope.

Christ as the Hope of Christians

From what we have said so far, it becomes apparent that Paul centers his hope on Christ. Christ is the basis of hope, and Christ in the present effectively carries out the realization of hope. The love of Christ who died for them assures the believers of his faithfulness to the end. The love of God *in Christ* assures them of God's faithfulness to the end. Christ's present lordship is his continuing salvific activity on their behalf (1 Cor 15:24–28), and the exalted Lord is now interceding on their behalf in heaven (Rom 8:34). Christ himself will come in the end-time and raise the dead, transform the present lowly bodies into the form of his own risen body, gather them around himself and present them to the Father (1 Cor 15:50–56; 2 Cor 4:14; 1 Thess 4:13–18). For Paul Christ is the fulfillment of all the promises of God (2 Cor 1:20; Rom 15:8). The believers are therefore to cling to Christ and, being in him, hope to be with him in the end-time. Christ is the hope of Christians. He is the desire of Paul's heart.

Through Christ in God

Yet Christ is the way to the Father. Hence it is God, the Father of Christ, who is for the apostle the ultimate hope of the faithful. Christ is never dissociated from the Father.

It is God's love, faithfulness and power that are manifested in the Christ event. Christ's death for us, as we have seen, is the expression of the unsurpassable love of God for us. Christ's resurrection is God's act on our behalf. It is God who gave to the risen Christ the power to carry out his salvific purpose. It is God who is, through Christ, leading us into his kingdom, sustaining us in our present trials and placing us in Christ. It is God who will not let any power or any happening in all creation separate us from his love. It is God who is, through his Holy Spirit, pouring into our hearts his love and reassuring us. The ultimate completion is the kingdom of God, when God will be ''everything to everyone'' (1 Cor 15:28). This is the purpose of the Christ-event. It is the Father whom the sons and daughters desire and to whom they belong. The Son leads the ''sons of God'' to the Father. The Father is the hope of Christians.

Conclusion

We have presented, in a sharper focus than usual, the basis, the aspiration, and the certainty of hope in Paul. We saw that the ultimate ground, support and goal of hope is God himself, yet the

God who manifests himself in the Christ event and in the activity of the Holy Spirit.

Christian hope is thus not a groundless hope. It is not a hope without hope. Nor is it merely a trust in the God who comes to us always from the future. Rather, the apostle's hope has a definite ultimate object: to be with Christ in the glory of God. This includes specifically the parousia of Christ and the end-time resurrection-transformation into the likeness of the risen Lord. However, the latter realities are not the ultimate goal, but a condition for reaching it (1 Cor 15:50).[4] Paul sees all this as the working out and the completion of the resurrection of Christ. He presents this as the binding exposition of his gospel, as resting on the knowledge of God (1 Cor 15:34).

Hope is thus not merely the openness of faith to the future, a freedom for the future, as Bultmann would have it.[5] It includes the parousia of Christ and the future resurrection modeled on that of Christ and expected through the intervention of Christ and the Spirit. It is not a remnant of Jewish apocalyptic, a mythological language which has to be reinterpreted. As Beker has pointed out, not every philosophical system can adequately reproduce and translate the apostle's thought. Against Bultmann Beker maintains that faith is not hope, but has hope.[6]

The subject of hope is the believer. The apostle expands the Old Testament and apocalyptic limitation of hope to Israel, according to which the Gentiles at best only shared in and acknowledged the prerogative and the glory of Israel. For Paul, hope is meant for all, Jews and Gentiles (Rom 15:8–13): all are called to believe on the same basis; all are given the same hope as sons of God. The entire creation will share in their liberation.

The fact that God in Christ grounds, sustains and realizes hope gives great relief to the believer. The faithful need not set their security on any human effort or goodness or fidelity but on the love, faithfulness and power of God. The believer is therefore borne along by the knowledge of the love of God in Christ and secure in its experience.

Hope is something very personal. Paul's desire is to be with Christ his Lord. Touched by the love of God and his Son the believer responds personally in love. Hope becomes the movement of the heart to personal union with Christ.

Because hope belongs to this life of faith, of the cross, of temptations, it involves patience (Rom 5:3), steadfastness (1 Thess 1:3), courage (2 Cor 4:16–18). The apostle never tires of encouraging and exhorting the faithful. He is aware of anxieties and of the need of constant mutual support. He himself, in his own trials has learned the comfort of God and shares it with others. He prays for those in his charge that they may persevere to the end. It is thus not surprising that hope is also associated with peace (Rom 15:13), joy (5:2), longing (2 Cor 5:2), glorification of God (Rom 15:6) and thanksgiving (2 Cor 1:11). Paul also shares these riches of hope with the faithful and prays that they may abound in hope.

From all this it becomes clear that Christian hope is not an escape from the problems and demands of this life, as the Marxists would have it. It gives meaning to and sustains suffering. It calls for an active engagement for the kingdom of God. Moltmann has called for the Christian social and political program.[7] It is not an escape into a utopia or a dreamland, which would deny the present harsh reality and abandon all moral effort.

Paul's hope is part and parcel of his eschatology, i.e., of his view of the end-time reality. According to Nebe, it is subsumed to eschatology, although the two depend on each other.[8]

This hope, given and sustained by God, remains very much a human hope and shares its characteristics. We do not as yet have an adequate philosophical and psychological explanation of it.[9] Hope is basically a matter of the heart. It enlivens the whole being, spirit as well as body. And since the whole being tends toward and yearns for completion, hope brings the expected fulfillment close to the present in time and space. It cannot acquiesce in separation. It foreshortens the distance and yearns to bridge the gap. The greater the hope, the more intense the expectation of its near fulfillment. This foreshortening results from the movement of love toward the beloved. The heart filled with love yearns to abide in the beloved and strives to bridge the distance.

It is for this reason that the apostle longed to die and be with the Lord (Phil 1:21–23). This also explains the early Christians' ardent expectation of the Lord's coming. Paul, contrary to the opinion of some scholars, never abandoned this lively expectation, even though it was probably tempered with the realization that he would die before the Lord's coming.

Conclusion

Our presentation of what they say about Paul contains critical information about some recent opinions concerning certain key aspects of the apostle's thought. It does not convey a general consensus, although the lines of it are indicated whenever possible. It includes our own view of Paul's theology as well. We found out that, although the apostle's experience at Damascus is not what he preached, it lent to his preaching and teaching a definite form and emphasis. It also gave him a profound knowledge of Christ, of God's plan of salvation, and of his own part in it. It shaped his life.

The Damascus event is not the only formative influence on Paul's theology. That cannot be understood apart from his Hellenistic milieu, his Jewish upbringing, the faith of the early Church and his other experiences, including visions. Yet the Damascus experience claims priority over all these as it was his direct encounter with the risen Christ that reversed his former values and made him an apostle of Christ.

The resurrection of Christ and its meaning belong to the very core of Paul's gospel. For him the resurrection of Christ is a fact attested by the appearances of the risen Jesus. As the texts indicate, he was scarcely concluding in a naive fashion to a resurrection of Jesus on the basis of an experience of seeing. We have pointed out some serious historical and exegetical reservations against such a view. Nor did the apostle himself or tradition before him refer to the resurrection appearances primarily as legitimations. It would be a perverse reading of the texts in question to maintain such a view. The meaning of the resurrection of Christ is the subject matter of the entire 1 Corinthians 15. Here the faith dimension of that event is most apparent. This interpretation cannot be derived from Jewish apocalyptic or from gnostic sources. Nor is it subject to our twentieth-century "enlightened" norms of what is believable. It has become apparent that Paul understood the end-time resurrection as a saving event in itself.

The ongoing discussion concerning justification by faith shows developments which may be of the greatest ecumenical significance. It was for this reason that we have incorporated here as many important contributions as possible. Although many aspects of the matter still need further clarification, the first lines of agreement are beginning to appear. Justification by faith is an important aspect of the apostle's theology, but scarcely its center.

The cross is Paul's theological understanding of the mode of Christ's death. He sees the latter as God's encountering the powers of evil in the world and worldly perspectives and values. The meaning of the cross cannot be isolated from the identity of Jesus, from his resurrection, lordship, and the final victory of God. The apostle draws from it personal and pastoral implications.

All these themes are somehow incorporated into hope which springs from the love, the faithfulness and the power of God manifested, for us, in Christ. From this the believer knows that what happened to Christ is to happen to those who belong to Christ. The emphasis here is on Christ's resurrection which embraces the resurrection of the faithful. It is in this reassurance that Paul calls on the faithful to become conformed to Christ and to accept the cross. It is in the hope of the resurrection that present sufferings appear slight in comparison with the glory to come.

There is a pastoral implication in all these themes. The apostle formulated his thought in response to the particular problems in his communities. In all of them he speaks as a chosen interpreter of Christ and as an obedient minister of grace. His sole intention is that that grace may extend to many to the praise and glory of God. May the reader share in that grace.

Notes

Chapter 1
Paul's Damascus Experience

1. B. Rigaux, *Letters of Paul. Modern Studies* (Chicago: Franciscan Herald, 1968) 42–55.

2. "The Key to Pauline Theology," *ExpTim* 76 (1964/65) 27–30.

3. J. Jeremias, "Key," 28.

4. See G. Bornkamm, *Paul-Paulus* (New York-Evanston: Harper & Row, 1971) 3–12.

5. Jeremias, "Key," 28.

6. Bornkamm, *Paul,* 9.

7. Jeremias, "Key," 28.

8. Bornkamm, *Paul,* 9.

9. This is held by D.M. Stanley, "Paul's Conversion in Acts: Why the Three Accounts?" CBQ 15 (1953) 315–38.

10. Implied by J. Jervell, *Luke and the People of God. A New Look at Luke-Acts* (Minneapolis: Augsburg, 1972) 162–63.

11. G. Lohfink, *The Conversion of Paul* (Chicago: Franciscan Herald, 1975).

12. J. Munck, *Paul and Salvation of Mankind* (Richmond: J. Knox, 1959).

13. For these opinions, see Rigaux, *Letters,* 60–62.

14. W. Marxsen, "The Resurrection of Jesus as a Historical and Theological Problem," *The Significance of the Message of the Resurrection for Faith in Jesus Christ* (ed. C.F.D. Moule; SBT 8; London: SCM, 1968) 15–50, esp. 35–37.

15. J.C. Beker, *Paul the Apostle. The Triumph of God in Life and Thought* (Philadelphia: Fortress, 1980) 183.

16. Ibid., 183.

17. W. Prokulski, "The Conversion of St. Paul," CBQ 19 (1957) 453–73.

18. Rigaux, *Letters,* 53.

19. See G. von Rad, *Old Testament Theology II* (New York: Harper, 1965) 50–55.

20. Rigaux, *Letters,* 61–62. For the opinions of P. Gaechter, L. Cerfaux, H. Schlier and others, see ibid., 58–61.

21. Beker, *Paul,* 5–7.

22. Ibid., 8.

23. Jeremias, "Key," 29–30.

24. Rigaux, *Letters,* 62.

25. See ibid., 64.

26. J. Fitzmyer, "Pauline Theology. A Brief Sketch," JBC II 800–27, esp. 805.

Chapter 2
The Resurrection of Christ

1. See J. Kloppenborg, "An Analysis of the Pre-Pauline Formula in 1 Cor 15:3b–5 in Light of Some Recent Literature," CBQ 40 (1978) 351–67; J. Murphy-O'Connor, "Tradition and Redaction in 1 Cor 15:3–7," CBQ 43 (1981) 582–89.

2. R. Bultmann, "A Reply to the Theses of J. Schniewind," *Kerygma and Myth. A Theological Debate* (ed. H.W. Bartsch; New York: Harper & Row, 1961) 102–23, esp. 112.

3. Quoted by R. Bultmann in "New Testament and Mythology," *Kerygma and Myth. A Theological Debate* (ed. H.W. Bartsch; New York: Harper & Row, 1961) 1–44, esp. 39.

4. U. Wilckens, "The Tradition-history of the Resurrection of Jesus," *The Significance of the Message of the Resurrection for Faith in Jesus Christ* (ed. C.F.D. Moule; SBT 8; London: SCM, 1968) 51–76.

5. R. Pesch, "Zur Entstehung des Glaubens an die Auferstehung Jesu. Ein Vorschlag zur Diskussion," TQ 153 (1973) 201–28.

6. Marxsen, "Resurrection," 15–50.
7. Ibid., 31.
8. Ibid., 36.
9. Ibid., 38.
10. Ibid., 40.
11. Wilckens, "Tradition-history," 62–66.
12. Ibid., 61–66.
13. Ibid., 66–67.

Chapter 3
The Meaning of Christ's Resurrection

1. P. Hoffman, *Die Toten in Christus. Eine religionsgeschichtliche und exegetische Untersuchung zur paulinischen Eschatologie* (NA 2; Münster: Aschendorff, 1966) 144–55, 341–44.
2. Hoffmann, *Toten*, 253–85.
3. Ibid., 286–320.
4. Ibid., 254–67, 296–301.
5. Beker, *Paul*, 81, 135, 356–67.
6. G. Greshake, *Auferstehung der Toten. Ein Beitrag zur gegenwärtigen theologischen Diskussion über die Zukunft der Geschichte* (Essen: Ludgerus Verlag H. Wingen, 1969) 52–95.
7. Ibid., 91–95.
8. Ibid., 88–91.
9. R. Bultmann, *Theology of the New Testament 1. The Message of Jesus. The Kerygma of the Earliest Church. The Theology of Paul* (London: SCM, 1952) 288–352.
10. Greshake, *Auferstehung*, 96–133.
11. Beker, *Paul*, 154.
12. Ibid.
13. J. Moltmann, *Theology of Hope. On the Ground and the Implications of a Christian Eschatology* (London: SCM, 1965). For a discussion of Moltmann's model of the resurrection, see Greshake, *Auferstehung*, 134–62.
14. G. Greshake – G. Lohfink, *Naherwartung-Auferstehung-Unsterblichkeit* (QD 71; Freiburg-Basel-Vienna: Herder, 1975) 38–91.

Chapter 4
Justification by Faith

1. N.A. Dahl, *Studies in Paul. Theology of the Early Christian Mission* (Minneapolis: Augsburg, 1977) 117.

2. E. Käsemann, "Gottesgerechtigkeit bei Paulus," ZTK 58 (1961) 367–78 (=*Exegetische Versuche und Besinnungen II*, 181–93).

3. Ibid.

4. E. Käsemann, *Commentary on Romans* (Grand Rapids: Eerdmans, 1980) 28.

5. Ibid., 29.

6. C. Müller, *Gottesgerechtigkeit und Gottes Volk. Eine Untersuchung zu Römer 9–11* (FRLANT 86; Göttingen: Vandenhoeck & Ruprecht, 1964) 202–36.

7. P. Stuhlmacher, *Gerechtigkeit Gottes bei Paulus* (FRLANT 87; 2d ed.; Göttingen: Vandenhoeck & Ruprecht, 1966).

8. K. Kertelge, *"Rechtfertigung" bei Paulus. Studien zur Struktur und zum Bedeutungsgehalt des paulinischen Rechtfertigungsbegriffs* (NA 3; Münster: Aschendorff, 1967).

9. Ibid., 107–09, 305–07.

10. Ibid., 15–62.

11. Ibid., 286–304.

12. Ibid., 306.

13. Ibid., 112–20.

14. Ibid., 306.

15. J.A. Ziesler, *The Meaning of Righteousness in Paul. A Linguistic and Theological Enquiry* (Cambridge: University Press, 1972).

16. Ibid., 147–48.

17. Ibid., 212.

18. Ibid., 192.

19. K. Stendahl, *Paul among Jews and Gentiles and Other Essays* (Philadelphia: Fortress, 1976).

20. *Studies*.

21. E.P. Sanders, *Paul and Palestinian Judaism. A Comparison of Patterns of Religion* (Philadelphia: Fortress, 1977).

22. Stendahl, *Paul*, 29.

23. Ibid., 33.
24. Dahl, *Studies,* 79–94.
25. Ibid., 74–78.
26. Ibid., 110–11.
27. Sanders, *Paul,* 12–24.
28. Ibid., 441–47.
29. Ibid., 456–72
30. Ibid., 495.
31. Ibid., 502–04.
32. Ibid., 501, 506.
33. H. Schlier, *Der Römerbrief* (HTKNT 6; Freiburg-Basel-Vienna: Herder, 1977).
34. U. Wilckens, *Der Brief an die Römer* (EKKNT 6/1; Zürich-Einsiedeln-Köln: Benziger; Neukirchen-Vluyn: Neukirchener, 1978).
35. Ziesler, *Meaning,* 168.
36. J. Reumann, *Righteousness in the New Testament. With Responses by Joseph A. Fitzmyer and Jerome D. Quinn* (Philadelphia: Fortress; New York-Ramsey: Paulist Press, 1982).

Chapter 5
The Cross

1. R. Tannehill, *Dying and Rising with Christ. A Study in Pauline Theology* (Berlin: Töpelmann, 1967) 14–20.
2. It is in associating the law with the powers of the old dominion that Paul's dualism differs from John's.
3. Tannehill, *Dying,* 17.
4. Beker, *Paul,* 204.
5. R. Schnackenburg, *Baptism in the Thought of St. Paul* (Oxford: Blackwell, 1964) 156–66.
6. Tannehill, *Dying,* 5, 21–43.
7. Bultmann, *Theology 1,* 302–03.
8. Beker, *Paul,* 189–92.
9. Ibid., 185.
10. Ibid., 184–89.
11. Sanders, *Paul,* 442–47.

12. Bultmann, *Theology 1*, 341.
13. S. Lyonnet, "St. Paul, Liberty and Law," The Bridge 4 (1962) 220–51.
14. Beker, *Paul*, 204.
15. Ibid., 199.
16. Ibid., 205.

Chapter 6
Hope

1. Beker, *Paul*, 147–49.
2. J. Plevnik, "The Taking up of the Faithful and the Resurrection of the Dead in 1 Thessalonians 4:13–18," CBQ (1984) 274–83.
3. R. Bultmann, "*elpis*," TDNT 2 (1964) 517–23.
4. G. Nebe, "*Hoffnung*" *bei Paulus. Elpis und ihre Synonyme im Zusammenhang der Eschatologie* (SUNT 16; Göttingen: Vandenhoeck & Ruprecht, 1983) 173.
5. Bultmann, *Theology 1*, 301–02.
6. Beker, *Paul*, 147, 170–73.
7. Moltmann, *Hope*.
8. G. Nebe, "*Hoffnung*," 174.
9. For a short discussion on this, see J. Macquarrie, *Christian Hope* (New York: Seabury, 1978) 1–30; also, *In Search of Humanity. A Theological and Philosophical Approach* (New York: Crossroad, 1983) 243–52. Macquarrie mentions Gabriel Marcel who spoke of a "metaphysic of hope" from the Christian perspective, and Ernst Bloch's *Prinzip der Hoffnung*, written from the neo-Marxist point of view.

Bibliography

Bartsch, H.W., ed., *Kerygma and Myth. A Theological Debate* (New York: Harper & Row, 1961).

Beker, J.C., *Paul the Apostle. The Triumph of God in Life and Thought* (Philadelphia: Fortess, 1980).

Bornkamm, G., *Paul-Paulus* (New York-Evanston: Harper & Row, 1971).

Bultmann, R., *Theology of the New Testament 1. The Message of Jesus. The Kerygma of the Earliest Church. The Theology of Paul* (London: SCM, 1952).

————, "A Reply to the Theses of J. Schniewind," *Kerygma and Myth. A Theological Debate* (ed. H.W. Bartsch; New York: Harper & Row, 1961).

————, "New Testament and Mythology," *Kerygma and Myth. A Theological Debate* (ed. H.W. Bartsch; New York: Harper & Row, 1961).

————, "*elpis*," TDNT 2 (1964) 517–23.

Dahl, N.A., *Studies in Paul. Theology of the Early Christian Mission* (Minneapolis: Augsburg, 1971).

Fitzmyer, J.A., "Pauline Theology. A Brief Sketch," JBC II 800–27.

Greshake, G., *Auferstehung der Toten. Ein Beitrag zur gegenwärtigen theologischen Diskussion über die Zukunft der Geschichte* (Essen: Ludgerus Verlag H. Wingen, 1966).

Greshake, G. – Lohfink, G., *Naherwartung-Auferstehung-Unsterblichkeit* (QD 71; Freiburg-Basel-Vienna: Herder, 1975).

Hoffmann, P., *Die Toten in Christus. Eine religionsgeschichtliche und exegetische Untersuchung zur paulinischen Eschatologie* (NA 2; Münster: Aschendorff, 1966).

Jeremias, J., "The Key to Pauline Theology," *ExpTim* 76(1964/65) 27–30.

Jervell, J., *Luke and the People of God. A New Look at Luke-Acts* (Minneapolis: Augsburg, 1972).

Käsemann, E., *Commentary on Romans* (Grand Rapids: Eerdmans, 1980).

———, "Gottesgerechtigkeit bei Paulus," ZTK 58 (1961) 367–78 (=Exegetische Versuche und Besinnungen II, 181–93).

Kertelge, K., *"Rechfertigung" bei Paulus. Studien zur Struktur und zum Bedeutungsgehalt des paulinischen Rechtfertigungsbefriffs* (NA 3; Münster: Aschendorff, 1967).

Kloppenborg, J., "An Analysis of the Pre-Pauline Formula in 1 Cor 15:3b–5 in Light of Some Recent Literature," CBQ 40 (1978) 351–67.

Lohfink, G., *The Conversion of Paul* (Chicago: Franciscan Herald, 1975).

Lyonnet, S., "St. Paul, Liberty and Law," The Bridge 4 (1962) 220–51.

Macquarrie, J., *Christian Hope* (New York: Seabury, 1978).

———, *In Search of Humanity. A Theological and Philosophical Approach* (New York: Crossroad, 1983).

Marxsen, W., "The Resurrection of Jesus as a Historical and Theological Problem," *The Significance of the Message of the Resurrection for Faith in Jesus Christ* (ed. C.F.D. Moule; SBT 8; London: SCM, 1968).

Moltmann, J., *Theology of Hope. On the Ground and the Implications of a Christian Eschatology* (London: SCM, 1965).

Müller, C., *Gottesgerechtigkeit und Gottes Volk. Eine Untersuchung zu Römer 9–11* (FRLANT 86; Göttingen: Vandenhoeck & Ruprecht, 1964).

Munck, J., *Paul and Salvation of Mankind* (Richmond: Knox, 1959).

Murphy-O'Connor, J., "Tradition and Redaction in 1 Cor 15:3–7," CBQ 43 (1981) 582–89.

Nebe, G., *"Hoffnung" bei Paulus. Elpis und ihre Synonyme im Zusam-*

menhang der Eschatologie (SUNT 16; Göttingen: Vandenhoeck & Ruprecht, 1983).

Pesch, R., ''Zur Entstehung des Glaubens an die Auferstehung Jesu. Ein Vorschlag zur Diskussion,'' TQ 153 (1973) 201–28.

Plevnik, J., ''The Taking up of the Faithful and the Resurrection of the Dead in 1 Thessalonians 4:13–18,'' CBQ 46 (1984) 274–83.

Prokulski, W., ''The Conversion of St. Paul,'' CBQ 19 (1957) 453–73.

von Rad, G., *Old Testament Theology II* (New York: Harper, 1965).

Reumann, J., *Righteousness in the New Testament. With Responses by Joseph A. Fitzmyer and Jerome D. Quinn* (Philadelphia: Fortress; New York-Ramsey: Paulist Press, 1982).

Rigaux, B., *Letters of Paul. Modern Studies* (Chicago: Franciscan Herald, 1968).

Sanders, E.P. *Paul and Palestinian Judaism. A Comparison of Patterns of Religion* (Philadelphia: Fortress, 1977).

Schlier, H., *Der Römerbrief* (HTKNT 6; Freiburg-Basel-Vienna: Herder, 1977).

Schnackenburg, R., *Baptism in the Thought of St. Paul* (Oxford: Blackwell, 1964).

Stanley, D.M., ''Paul's Conversion in Acts: Why the Three Accounts?'' CBQ 15 (1953) 315–38.

Stendahl, K., *Paul among Jews and Gentiles and Other Essays* (Philadelphia: Fortress, 1976).

Stuhlmacher, P., *Gerechtigkeit Gottes bei Paulus* (FRLANT 87; 2d ed.; Göttingen: Vandenhoeck & Ruprecht, 1966).

Tannehill, R., *Dying and Rising with Christ. A Study in Pauline Theology* (Berlin: Töpelmann, 1967).

Wilckens, U., *Der Brief an die Römer* (EKKNT 6/1; Zürich-Einsiedeln-Köln: Benziger; Neukirchen-Vluyn: Neukirchener, 1978).

———, ''The Tradition-history of the Resurrection of Jesus,'' *The Significance of the Message of the Resurrection for Faith in Jesus Christ* (ed. C.F.D. Moule; SBT 8; London: SCM, 1968) 51–76.

Ziesler, J.A., *The Meaning of Righteousness in Paul. A Linguistic and Theological Enquiry* (Cambridge: University Press, 1972).

Other Books in this Series